BASIC BIBLE DOCTRINES

OF THE CHRISTIAN FAITH

EXPLAINING THE DOCTRINE OF LAST THINGS

Edward D. Andrews

EXPLAINING THE DOCTRINE OF LAST THINGS

Basic Bible Doctrines of the Christian Faith

Edward D. Andrews

Christian Publishing House
Cambridge, Ohio

EXPLAINING THE DOCTRINE OF LAST THINGS: Basic Bible Doctrines of the Christian Faith by Edward D. Andrews

ISBN-13: 978-0692669891

ISBN-10: 0692669892

Table of Contents

PREFACE

Few areas of Bible doctrine have suffered more from confusion, sensationalism, and human speculation than the doctrine of last things. Prophecy is often handled either as a field for endless guesswork or as a subject so difficult that ordinary Christians feel compelled to leave it to specialists, systems, and popular teachers. Yet Scripture never treats these matters as optional curiosities. Jehovah gave prophetic revelation for the strengthening of faith, the warning of the careless, the steadying of the troubled, and the encouragement of His people to live in holiness, courage, and hope. The last things are not given to satisfy restless speculation, but to show that history is moving under divine sovereignty toward a fixed and righteous conclusion. This book has been written with that conviction in mind.

The purpose of this volume is to explain the major doctrines of biblical eschatology in a clear, orderly, and text-governed way. The subject is far too important to be left to religious imagination, theological fashion, or systems that force the Scriptures into predetermined conclusions. The faithful student of the Bible must ask what the inspired writers meant in their historical setting, according to the grammar of the text, the literary form employed, and the wider testimony of Scripture. For that reason, this book approaches prophecy by the historical-grammatical method. It seeks to let Daniel speak as Daniel, Jesus speak as Jesus, Paul speak as Paul, Peter speak as Peter, and John speak as John, while also honoring the unity of the whole inspired canon. Prophecy is not a coded puzzle to be manipulated by modern theories. It is revelation from God, and it must be handled with reverence, restraint, and submission to the text.

In these chapters, the reader will move through the core themes that shape the Bible's teaching on the end of the age. We begin with the nature of prophecy itself, because no one can understand the last things rightly without first understanding what prophecy is and how it should be interpreted. From there, we consider the signs of the end of the age, the antichrist, the man of lawlessness, the mark of the beast, the great tribulation, and Armageddon. We then turn to doctrines that have often been distorted by tradition and emotionalism, including the so-called rapture, the nature of death, the biblical doctrine of hell, and the resurrection hope. Finally, we consider the millennium, the final rebellion, the great white throne, the final judgment, the question of the unevangelized, and the glorious promise of the new heavens and new earth. This order reflects the broad scope and progression of the book as it appears in your manuscript.

A matter of special importance should be stated plainly at the outset. This book does not approach eschatology as though the Christian's task were to master a chart, identify every current event, or force prophecy into newspaper interpretation. Nor does it treat last things as an abstract theological field detached from Christian living. The Bible's doctrine of last things is pastoral, moral, and doxological. It teaches that Jehovah governs history, that Jesus Christ will openly triumph, that evil is temporary, that death will be abolished, that judgment is certain, and that the faithful must endure in truth until the end. Prophecy should therefore deepen reverence for God, sharpen discernment, strengthen resolve, and enlarge hope. It should not make believers unstable, fearful, or obsessed with speculative detail. When rightly understood, the doctrine of last things does not weaken Christian faithfulness in the present; it intensifies it.

This volume also proceeds from several biblical convictions that must remain fixed if the doctrine of last things is to be explained coherently. Scripture is the inspired, inerrant, and infallible Word of God. Its prophecies are truthful, meaningful, and certain in their fulfillment. The dead are truly dead and await resurrection. Eternal life is the gift of God, not the natural possession of man. Final judgment is real, the second death is real, and the wicked do not inherit the kingdom of God. Jesus Christ is central to every part of eschatology, not merely as one figure among many, but as the One through whom Jehovah brings His redemptive purpose to completion. He is the risen Lord, the coming Judge, the victorious King, and the Lamb through whom the faithful receive life. Any approach to last things that marginalizes Christ, distorts the biblical doctrine of death and resurrection, or places human tradition above Scripture will inevitably go astray.

My aim in writing this book is therefore both theological and practical. I want the reader to understand what the Bible actually teaches, to be protected against popular error, and to stand more firmly in the truth. I also want the reader to see that the last things are not a dark and confusing appendix to Christian doctrine, but a radiant declaration of Jehovah's justice, Christ's victory, and the certainty of the kingdom. The end of the present age is not the collapse of divine purpose. It is the overthrow of rebellion. The return of Christ is not a vague religious symbol. It is a real and decisive intervention in history. The resurrection hope is not sentimental language. It is the answer of God to death. The final judgment is not a mere metaphor for accountability. It is the public and irreversible vindication of divine righteousness. And the new heavens and new earth are not wishful thinking. They are the consummation of all that Jehovah purposed from the beginning.

If this book helps readers turn away from prophetic speculation and toward biblical clarity, if it helps them reject false teaching and hold fast to the apostolic faith, if it strengthens them to endure in a fallen world, and if it fixes their hope more firmly on the coming triumph of God and of His Christ, then it will have served its purpose well. May Jehovah bless your study of His Word, deepen your confidence in His promises, and strengthen you to live faithfully in these last days as you await the full outworking of all that He has spoken.

Edward D. Andrews

Author of over 220 books and Chief Translator of the Updated American Standard Version (UASV)

INTRODUCTION

The doctrine of last things—often called eschatology—addresses the final stage of Jehovah's purpose for mankind and the world. It concerns the end of the present age, the return of Christ, the defeat of evil, the resurrection of the dead, the final judgment, and the establishment of the new heavens and the new earth. These subjects are not peripheral matters within the Christian faith. They stand at the culmination of the entire biblical narrative. From Genesis to Revelation, Scripture moves steadily toward the moment when God brings His redemptive purpose to completion and establishes His righteous rule without opposition.

Despite its importance, the doctrine of last things is frequently misunderstood. Many approach biblical prophecy as though it were a field for speculation, where imagination and current events are used to construct elaborate theories about the future. Others avoid the subject entirely, assuming that prophecy is too complex or symbolic to be understood. Both approaches miss the purpose for which Jehovah gave prophetic revelation. The prophetic portions of Scripture were not written to satisfy curiosity or to encourage endless speculation. They were given so that God's people might understand the direction of history, remain faithful in the face of opposition, and live with confident hope in the certainty of God's promises.

The Bible presents history as purposeful and directed. It is not a random sequence of events without meaning. Jehovah is the Creator of heaven and earth, and He governs history according to His will. Isaiah 46:9-10 records His declaration: "I am God, and there is no other; I am God, and there is none like me, declaring the end from the beginning and from ancient times things not yet done." The doctrine of last things therefore reveals the goal toward which God has been moving history from the beginning. What Scripture announces about the future is not uncertain prediction but divine revelation. The same God who created the world and guided the history of Israel has also declared how the present age will end and what will follow it.

To understand these matters correctly, the reader must approach prophecy with careful attention to the text of Scripture. The Bible must be interpreted according to the historical-grammatical method, which seeks to understand what the inspired writers meant in their historical setting and according to the normal meaning of their words. Prophetic passages often contain vivid imagery and symbolic language, but the presence of symbolism does not mean the message is uncertain or unknowable. Symbols were used by the biblical writers to communicate real events and realities. When those symbols are interpreted within their scriptural context, the meaning becomes clear.

Throughout this book, prophecy will therefore be examined in light of the broader testimony of Scripture. No single passage should be isolated from the rest of the Bible. The teachings of Daniel, Jesus, Paul, Peter, and John form a unified witness regarding the future. When these writings are studied together, they provide a coherent picture of the events that lead to the end of the present age and the establishment of God's final kingdom.

A central truth that emerges from biblical prophecy is that the present world is temporary in its current form. Scripture repeatedly teaches that the age in which we now live is marked by sin, rebellion, deception, and death. These realities are not permanent features of

God's purpose. They are the result of mankind's fall into sin and the continuing influence of a wicked world system opposed to God. The Bible does not present the present condition of the world as something that will gradually improve through human progress. Instead, it teaches that God Himself will intervene decisively in history to bring about the end of the present order.

Jesus spoke about this future intervention when His disciples asked Him about the end of the age. In Matthew 24:3 they asked, "Tell us, when will these things be, and what will be the sign of your coming and of the end of the age?" Jesus' response described a period characterized by deception, conflict, persecution, and increasing lawlessness. These events do not signal that God has lost control of history. Rather, they reveal that history is moving toward a divinely appointed conclusion. The end of the age will not come through human planning or political reform. It will come through the direct action of God.

The New Testament writers consistently connect the end of the age with the return of Jesus Christ. Acts 1:11 records the angelic declaration given to the disciples after Jesus' ascension: "This Jesus, who was taken up from you into heaven, will come in the same way as you saw him go into heaven." The return of Christ is therefore not symbolic language for spiritual renewal or moral progress. It is a real and future event in which the risen Lord will return openly to bring judgment upon the wicked and deliverance to the faithful.

The return of Christ also leads directly to the resurrection of the dead. Death is one of the most universal realities of human existence. Every generation experiences its sorrow and finality. Yet Scripture teaches that death does not have the final word. Jesus declared in John 5:28-29 that "all who are in the tombs will hear his voice and come out." The resurrection is God's answer to death. It is the moment when those who have died are raised by divine power to face either everlasting life or final judgment.

The resurrection is closely connected with the doctrine of final judgment. The Bible teaches that all people will ultimately stand before God to give an account of their lives. Revelation 20:12 describes the scene in vivid terms: "And I saw the dead, great and small, standing before the throne, and books were opened." The final judgment reveals the perfect justice of Jehovah. Those who have rejected Him and lived in rebellion will face the second death, while those who belong to Him will receive the gift of everlasting life.

The end of judgment is not destruction alone but renewal. Revelation 21:1 declares, "Then I saw a new heaven and a new earth." This statement summarizes the final goal of God's redemptive purpose. The present order of sin, suffering, and death will pass away, and a new order will take its place. In that new creation, God will dwell with His people, death will be abolished, and the former sorrows of human life will be gone. Revelation 21:4 promises that God "will wipe away every tear from their eyes, and death shall be no more."

This hope stands at the heart of the Christian message. The gospel does not merely promise forgiveness of sins in the present life. It promises participation in the future kingdom of God and the restoration of creation itself. The new heavens and new earth represent the final answer to the problem of sin and death that entered the world in the beginning.

The chapters that follow explore the major themes of biblical eschatology in a systematic way. We will examine the nature of prophecy, the signs that mark the approach of the end of the age, the rise of the antichrist and the man of lawlessness, the meaning of the mark of the beast, the period known as the great tribulation, and the climactic conflict often referred to as Armageddon. We will also consider the biblical teaching about death, the resurrection hope, the final judgment, the millennium, and the eternal destiny of mankind.

These subjects are not presented to encourage fear or speculation. They are given so that believers may understand the certainty of God's promises and live with steadfast faith. The doctrine of last things reminds us that the present age is temporary and that the kingdom of God will ultimately prevail. It assures us that injustice will not endure forever, that evil will be judged, and that righteousness will be established.

For the Christian, the study of prophecy should lead to greater devotion and faithfulness. Knowing that history is moving toward the return of Christ should inspire believers to remain steadfast in their loyalty to God. It should also deepen our appreciation for the salvation that has been provided through Jesus Christ. The same Lord who died for the sins of the world will one day return to establish His righteous kingdom.

The doctrine of last things therefore calls every reader to thoughtful reflection. It confronts us with the reality that history is moving toward a divinely appointed conclusion and that every person must consider his relationship with God. Those who belong to Christ can look forward to the fulfillment of God's promises with confidence and hope. Those who ignore or reject God's revelation face the certainty of His judgment.

As you begin this study, the goal is not merely to learn about future events but to understand the message that God has revealed about the completion of His purpose. The Bible presents the end of the age as the moment when God's justice, mercy, and truth will be fully displayed. The triumph of Christ, the resurrection of the dead, the judgment of evil, and the renewal of creation together form the final chapter of God's redemptive work.

The pages that follow seek to explain these truths carefully and faithfully from the Scriptures. By examining what the Bible actually teaches about the last things, we can approach the future not with uncertainty or fear, but with confidence in the One who declares the end from the beginning and who will surely bring His purpose to completion.

CHAPTER 1 Explaining Biblical Prophecy

The Nature of Biblical Prophecy

Biblical prophecy is not religious guesswork, poetic exaggeration, or a coded system meant to satisfy human curiosity. It is revelation from Jehovah. The prophets did not speak from private insight, political instinct, or imaginative reflection. They spoke because God made known to them what human beings could not discover by their own wisdom. Peter makes this plain when he writes that no prophecy of Scripture originates in the prophet's own interpretation, for prophecy was not produced by the will of man, but men spoke from God as they were carried along by the Holy Spirit (2 Pet. 1:20-21). That statement establishes the foundation for every right understanding of prophecy. Prophecy begins with God, not man. It is divine disclosure, not human invention.

For that reason, prophecy must never be treated as a playground for speculation. The same God who inspired prophecy also determined its meaning. The task of the interpreter is not to force prophecy into modern theories, emotional fears, or speculative systems, but to ask what the inspired writer meant by the words that he used in the context in which he wrote them. Isaiah, Jeremiah, Ezekiel, Daniel, Zechariah, Jesus, Paul, Peter, and John each wrote in real historical settings, using meaningful language, speaking to real people, and addressing real covenant realities. Their words may reach far beyond their own day, but they do not cease to have stable meaning because they speak of the future. Prophecy is still language, and language still communicates according to grammar, context, and authorial intention.

This is why biblical prophecy must be approached with reverence and restraint. Reverence is necessary because prophecy is the Word of God. Restraint is necessary because prophecy is not given to answer every question people may wish to ask. Jehovah reveals what He chooses to reveal, and He often leaves matters unspoken that He has not appointed for human knowledge. Deuteronomy 29:29 states that the hidden things belong to Jehovah our God, but the things revealed belong to us and to our sons forever. That principle applies forcefully to prophecy. The revealed things are sufficient for faith, obedience, endurance, and hope. The hidden things are not ours to invent.

Prophecy also differs from mere prediction. It can include prediction, and often does, but prophecy is larger than foretelling future events. The prophet proclaims divine truth. Sometimes prophecy exposes present sin. Sometimes it warns of coming judgment. Sometimes it comforts the faithful with promises of deliverance. Sometimes it interprets current events in the light of Jehovah's covenant. Sometimes it unveils the long-range course of history under divine rule. Because of that, prophecy should not be reduced to a timetable. It is moral, theological, covenantal, and often judicial. It tells people what God is doing, why He is doing it, and what response He requires.

The Purpose of Prophecy in Scripture

The purpose of prophecy is not to entertain curiosity about the future. It is to strengthen faith in the sovereignty of Jehovah, to call His people to obedience, and to assure them that history moves under His decree toward His appointed end. Isaiah repeatedly contrasts Jehovah with idols by stressing His power to declare the end from the beginning and from ancient times things not yet done (Isa. 46:9-10). In other words, prophecy is one of the ways God reveals that He alone is God. False gods cannot declare the future because they do not govern it. Jehovah declares it because He rules it.

This means prophecy is deeply connected to worship. When God foretells judgment and then brings it to pass, He vindicates His holiness. When He promises deliverance and then fulfills it, He vindicates His faithfulness. When He reveals the rise and fall of kingdoms before they appear, He shows that kings do not govern history independently of Him. Daniel 2 and 7 are central here. The succession of empires is not presented as random political development. It is disclosed beforehand to show that the Most High rules in the kingdom of men and gives it to whom He will (Dan. 4:17, 25, 32). The point is not merely that Daniel knows the future, but that Jehovah governs the future.

Prophecy also serves the faithful by preparing them for what lies ahead. Jesus told His disciples certain things beforehand so that when they took place they would believe (John 14:29). He warned them of false christs, tribulation, apostasy, and the coming of the Son of Man so that they would not be misled (Matt. 24:4-5, 11, 23-27). Prophecy therefore protects believers from panic. When properly understood, it teaches that evil does not arise outside the knowledge of God, suffering does not cancel His rule, and opposition to the truth is not proof that His purpose has failed. It is because prophecy shows the plan of God that believers can endure the pressure of the present age without surrendering to fear.

At the same time, prophecy exposes the moral seriousness of human response. Prophetic warnings are not empty declarations. They call for repentance, watchfulness, and obedience. Jonah announced coming judgment upon Nineveh, and the city humbled itself before God. The prophets warned Judah and Israel repeatedly, not because judgment was unreal, but because Jehovah is righteous and calls sinners to turn from their ways. Even when prophecy speaks of events that are fixed in the decree of God, it is never detached from moral accountability. Men are not spectators in a prophetic drama. They are answerable to the God who speaks.

The Difference Between True Prophecy and False Prophecy

Scripture draws a sharp line between true prophecy and false prophecy. A true prophet speaks in Jehovah's name and according to Jehovah's revelation. A false prophet speaks from his own heart, from demonic influence, or from a desire to please men. Jeremiah confronted prophets who spoke visions of their own minds and not from the mouth of Jehovah (Jer. 23:16). Ezekiel condemned those who followed their own spirit and had seen nothing (Ezek. 13:3). The issue was not merely factual error. It was rebellion against divine authority. False prophecy misrepresents God.

That distinction remains crucial because false prophecy often imitates the language of true religion. False prophets say, "Peace," when there is no peace (Jer. 6:14). They promise safety to people walking in rebellion. They speak flattering things, soothe consciences, and give the appearance of spiritual certainty while denying the truth. In the New Testament, Jesus warns of false prophets who come in sheep's clothing but inwardly are ravenous wolves (Matt. 7:15). Paul warns that savage wolves will arise, speaking twisted things to draw away disciples after themselves (Acts 20:29-30). John commands believers to test the spirits because many false prophets have gone out into the world (1 John 4:1).

The test of true prophecy is not emotional effect, public influence, or dramatic style. It is fidelity to the revelation of God. Deuteronomy 13 teaches that even if a sign or wonder occurs, a prophet must be rejected if he leads people away from Jehovah. Deuteronomy 18 teaches that a prophet who presumes to speak a word Jehovah has not commanded must not be feared. In the New Testament, the test becomes even more pointed around Jesus Christ. John says the spirit that confesses Jesus Christ as having come in the flesh is from God, but the spirit that does not confess Jesus is not from God; this is the spirit of the antichrist (1 John 4:2-3). Prophecy that denies the Son is not from the Father.

This means the study of prophecy cannot be separated from doctrine. A person may speak often about end times, tribulation, the beast, and signs, and still be profoundly false if his teaching corrupts the truth about God and Christ. Prophecy is not measured by excitement but by truth. That is why all claims about future events must remain under the authority of the whole biblical witness. A prophetic teacher who contradicts the plain teaching of Scripture is not made trustworthy by dramatic interpretation.

The Historical-Grammatical Meaning of Prophecy

Because prophecy is God-given language, it must be interpreted according to the ordinary principles by which meaningful language communicates. This is often called the historical-grammatical method. The phrase may sound technical, but the idea is simple. Words have meaning in context. Grammar matters. History matters. Literary form matters. Authorial intention matters. A prophecy does not mean whatever later readers imagine it to mean. It means what the inspired writer intended by the words he used in the setting in which he wrote.

This does not flatten prophecy into mere prose. Prophecy often includes poetry, symbolism, visions, and apocalyptic imagery. Yet even symbols signify according to context. Daniel's beasts are not literal zoological creatures, but neither are they shapeless symbols that can mean anything. Daniel 7 itself explains that the beasts are kings or kingdoms arising from the earth. Revelation's dragon is symbolic, yet Revelation 12 explicitly identifies the dragon as Satan. The symbolic form does not destroy meaning; it communicates meaning in a vivid and concentrated way. The interpreter's duty is to ask what the sign signifies according to the text itself and according to the broader scriptural patterns upon which the text depends.

For that reason, Scripture must interpret Scripture. Prophetic language in Revelation depends heavily on Daniel, Ezekiel, Zechariah, Isaiah, Exodus, and Genesis. The beast, the horns, the heavenly court, the plagues, the measuring, the harvest, the winepress, Gog and Magog, the New Jerusalem, and the tree of life all arise from earlier revelation. Revelation does not invent these themes in isolation. It gathers them into climactic form. The same is true of Jesus' teaching in Matthew 24, Mark 13, and Luke 21. His references to the abomination of desolation, unparalleled tribulation, and the Son of Man coming with the clouds are rooted in Daniel. A reader who ignores Daniel will misread Jesus, and a reader who severs Revelation from Daniel will almost certainly drift into confusion.

The historical setting also matters. Isaiah addressed Judah under threat. Jeremiah spoke in the final years before Jerusalem's fall. Ezekiel ministered among exiles. Daniel served under Babylonian and Persian rule. Haggai and Zechariah spoke after the return from exile. Jesus spoke under Roman occupation. Paul wrote to congregations facing pressure from false teachers and pagan culture. John addressed seven real congregations in Asia under the shadow of imperial power. These settings are not incidental details. They shape the meaning of the prophetic word. God spoke into real situations, and the future He revealed was disclosed through those settings, not detached from them.

The Place of Symbolism in Biblical Prophecy

A great deal of confusion about prophecy arises from failure to distinguish literal referent from symbolic presentation. Biblical prophecy uses imagery, visions, numbers, figures, and pictures because these forms communicate theological truth with force and depth. But symbolic language is not permission for imaginative freedom. Symbols are governed by the text.

For example, when Daniel sees four beasts coming up from the sea (Dan. 7:3), the sea represents the troubled realm of nations and human unrest, and the beasts represent kingdoms marked by predatory, anti-God character. The point is not zoology but empire. When Revelation speaks of a beast rising from the sea (Rev. 13:1), it draws on Daniel's established pattern of beastly world power. The beast is not every government in the abstract, nor is it any political figure each generation happens to fear. It is the mature anti-God political order in the context of the final conflict revealed in the Apocalypse.

Likewise, the mark of the beast is symbolic, but it points to something real. Revelation does not present the mark as an empty metaphor. It signifies allegiance, identity, and participation in a beastly order opposed to God. The symbolism does not erase the seriousness of the reality. Rather, it shows that the ultimate issue is worship and loyalty, not merely external mechanism. The same is true of Babylon the Great. She is symbolic, but she is not therefore unreal. She signifies the organized world system of idolatry, luxury, corruption, and persecution set against Jehovah and His people.

Numbers also carry symbolic force. Seven often signifies completeness, twelve covenant fullness, ten a large or full measure, and six falling short of divine completeness. Yet even here, symbolic force does not cancel real referent. The one thousand years of Revelation 20 must be read according to the context in which John places it, after the appearing of Christ in judgment and before the final rebellion and great white throne. The sequence matters. Symbolism cannot be used to dissolve structure whenever structure becomes inconvenient.

Prophecy and the Sovereignty of Jehovah

At the heart of biblical prophecy stands the absolute sovereignty of Jehovah. He does not react to history as though man controls it and He merely responds. He ordains times and seasons, raises up kings and removes them, and directs the course of kingdoms toward His appointed end. Daniel praises God because He changes times and seasons; He removes kings and sets up kings (Dan. 2:21). Nebuchadnezzar learns through humiliation that the Most High rules the kingdom of mankind and gives it to whom He will (Dan. 4:32). Cyrus is named in Isaiah before his birth as the one through whom God will accomplish His purpose for Jerusalem (Isa. 44:28; 45:1). The rise of Persia, the advance of Greece, the division of kingdoms, and the final arrogant ruler are all foreseen in Daniel because God governs them.

This is why prophecy gives comfort. It does not promise an easy path for the faithful in the present age. Indeed, prophecy repeatedly warns of tribulation, apostasy, deception, and persecution. But it shows that none of these realities are ultimate. Evil is active, but measured. Beastly power is real, but temporary. Satan deceives, but only within limits set by God. The antichristic order rises, but only to meet destruction at the appearing of Christ. Revelation makes this clear by showing judgments proceeding from heaven, the beast receiving authority only as it is given, Babylon remembered before God, and Satan finally cast into judgment.

The sovereignty of Jehovah also means that prophecy is not open-ended uncertainty. The future belongs to God. The return of Christ is certain. The resurrection is certain. Judgment is certain. The overthrow of evil is certain. The new heavens and new earth are certain. This certainty does not remove human responsibility, but it does remove despair. The people of God do not live in suspense over whether righteousness will triumph. They live in hope because Jehovah has spoken.

Prophecy and the Person of Jesus Christ

All biblical prophecy reaches its center in Jesus Christ. He is not merely one figure within prophecy. He is the One in whom the prophetic purpose of God comes to focus. The testimony of Jesus is the spirit of prophecy (Rev. 19:10). The prophets foretold the sufferings of Christ and the glories that would follow (1 Pet. 1:10-11). Jesus Himself taught that the Scriptures testify concerning Him (John 5:39). After His resurrection, He explained to His disciples the things concerning Himself in Moses, the Prophets, and the Psalms (Luke 24:27, 44-47).

This Christ-centered focus must govern the interpretation of prophecy. Prophecy is not mainly about modern politics, current anxieties, or speculative charts. It is about God's kingdom purpose in His Son. Daniel's Son of Man receiving dominion points to Him (Dan. 7:13-14). Isaiah's Servant songs find fulfillment in Him. Zechariah's pierced one points to Him (Zech. 12:10; John 19:37). The stone rejected by builders becomes the chief cornerstone in Him (Ps. 118:22; Acts 4:11). The Lamb in Revelation stands at the center of heaven's throne room because He alone is worthy to open the scroll and execute God's purpose (Rev. 5:1-10).

The same is true in eschatology. The antichrist is anti-Christ because he opposes the Son. The man of lawlessness exalts himself in the place that belongs to God and His Christ (2 Thess. 2:3-4). The beast wars against the Lamb and His people (Rev. 17:14). The great tribulation is followed by the appearing of the Son of Man (Matt. 24:29-31). The resurrection of the righteous is bound to Christ's victory over death (1 Cor. 15:20-26). The millennium is His reign. The final judgment is carried out under His authority (John 5:22, 27-29). The new creation is illuminated by the glory of God and the Lamb (Rev. 21:23). Prophecy, rightly understood, exalts Christ from beginning to end.

The Last Days, the Time of the End, and the Day of Jehovah

Biblical prophecy uses time expressions carefully, and these must not be confused. The "last days" refer to the final epoch of redemptive history inaugurated by the Messiah's first coming, death, resurrection, and exaltation. Peter applies Joel's prophecy of the last days to the apostolic age (Acts 2:16-17). Hebrews says God has spoken in these last days by His Son (Heb. 1:2). The church, therefore, has lived in the last days since the ascension of Christ.

Within that larger period, Daniel speaks of "the time of the end" (Dan. 8:17; 11:35, 40; 12:4, 9). This is not simply a synonym for the whole church age. It marks the concentrated final phase in which prophetic conflict intensifies and God's decree moves rapidly toward consummation. Daniel 12 associates it with unparalleled distress, Michael's intervention, deliverance for God's people, and resurrection. Jesus' Olivet Discourse follows this Danielic pattern. He speaks of the abomination of desolation, great tribulation, deception, heavenly signs, and the coming of the Son of Man (Matt. 24:15-31). Paul's teaching on the man of lawlessness and the appearing of Christ fits the same structure (2 Thess. 2:1-8).

Closely related is the Day of Jehovah, the day of the Lord. In Scripture this expression often denotes a decisive time of divine intervention in judgment and deliverance. It can refer to historical judgments in prophetic books, but in its fullest eschatological sense it points to the period of Christ's judicial manifestation and kingdom administration. The New Testament warns that the day of the Lord comes like a thief upon the unwatchful (1 Thess. 5:2-3; 2 Pet. 3:10). Revelation unfolds this day in its final and climactic dimensions. The churches live in the last days. The time of the end marks the intensified final crisis. The Day of Jehovah brings decisive intervention, judgment, and kingdom fulfillment.

These distinctions matter because prophecy is often confused by flattening all time language into one vague category. Scripture is more precise than that. The broad final era has already begun, the concentrated climax still lies ahead, and the Day of Jehovah brings God's decisive acts into full manifestation.

The Moral Demands of Prophecy

Prophecy is never given merely to inform the mind. It addresses the life. Because prophecy reveals what God is doing, it demands a response. Jesus repeatedly links prophecy to watchfulness. Since no one knows the day or hour of His return, His disciples must stay awake, remain ready, and be faithful servants (Matt. 24:42-51; 25:13). Paul says believers should not sleep as others do, but keep awake and stay sober because the day of the Lord will overtake the world unexpectedly (1 Thess. 5:4-8). Peter argues that since all these things are to be dissolved, believers ought to be persons of holy conduct and godliness, waiting for and hastening the coming of the day of God (2 Pet. 3:11-12).

This shows that prophecy has ethical force. It calls for purity, steadfastness, courage, and worship. Revelation blesses the one who reads, hears, and keeps the words of the prophecy (Rev. 1:3). The book was given to churches, not to speculative hobbyists. It warns compromising congregations, strengthens suffering congregations, and calls all of them to conquer through faithfulness. The issue is never mere awareness of events. It is loyalty to God and the Lamb under pressure.

Prophecy also guards against worldliness. When Scripture unveils the beastly character of worldly empire, the corruption of Babylon, and the final collapse of human pride, it teaches believers not to admire the present age as though it were the source of lasting security. The kingdoms of men appear strong, but they are temporary. Babylon appears rich, but she falls in one hour (Rev. 18:10, 17, 19). The beast appears triumphant, but the Lamb conquers him (Rev. 17:14). Those who understand prophecy rightly cannot give their hearts to a world under judgment.

The Hope Given by Prophecy

Although prophecy contains severe warnings, its final tone for the faithful is hope. Prophecy reveals judgment because evil is real and God is holy. But it also reveals victory because Jehovah does not abandon His purpose. Already in Genesis 3:15 the conflict between the woman's seed and the serpent points toward eventual triumph. The promises to Abraham, the covenant with David, the prophets' vision of the kingdom, the resurrection hope in Daniel 12, the teaching of Jesus, and the final visions of Revelation all move toward one conclusion: God will remove evil, vindicate the faithful, raise the dead, judge the wicked, and establish everlasting righteousness.

The hope of prophecy is therefore not escape into vagueness, nor survival of an immortal soul apart from the body. It is resurrection, kingdom, judgment, and restoration. Isaiah speaks of death being swallowed up forever (Isa. 25:8). Daniel speaks of many sleeping in the dust awakening, some to everlasting life and some to shame and everlasting contempt (Dan. 12:2). Jesus declares that all in the memorial tombs will hear His voice and come out, those who did good to a resurrection of life and those who practiced vile things to a resurrection of judgment (John 5:28-29). Paul teaches that Christ must reign until He has put all enemies under His feet, and the last enemy to be abolished is death (1 Cor. 15:25-26). Revelation shows the first resurrection, the thousand-year reign, the great white throne, the lake of fire which is the second death, and finally the new heaven and new earth where death is no more (Rev. 20:4-15; 21:1-4).

This is why prophecy should produce confidence rather than confusion in those who belong to God. It does not hide the severity of the conflict, but it makes clear that the outcome is fixed. The final word does not belong to antichristic rebellion, beastly dominion, lawlessness, war, or death. It belongs to Jehovah and to His Christ.

Reading Prophecy with Reverence and Clarity

A right approach to prophecy requires several commitments held together. First, prophecy must be read as the inspired Word of God. Second, it must be interpreted according to grammar, context, and scriptural usage. Third, symbols must be understood as meaningful signs, not as excuses for uncontrolled imagination. Fourth, prophecy must be read in continuity with the whole canon, especially with the patterns established in earlier revelation. Fifth, its moral purpose must never be separated from its predictive content. Sixth, its center must remain Jesus Christ and the kingdom purpose of Jehovah.

When these commitments are ignored, prophecy becomes distorted. Some reduce it to symbolism without historical substance. Others turn it into sensational forecasting detached from the text. Some flatten every prophetic enemy into one careless label. Others separate passages that Scripture itself joins. Still others obsess over timetables while neglecting holiness and endurance. None of these approaches does justice to the prophetic Word.

But when prophecy is read rightly, its effect is powerful and steadying. It humbles human pride because it shows that God governs history. It strengthens the faithful because it shows that suffering is measured and temporary. It sharpens discernment because it exposes deception before it comes in full force. It deepens worship because it reveals the glory of God and the centrality of His Son. It enlarges hope because it points beyond the present age of rebellion to the resurrection, the kingdom, and the restored creation.

Biblical prophecy, then, is not given to make the faithful restless with speculation. It is given to make them steadfast in truth. It is not given to produce fear of the future, but confidence in the God who has declared the future. It is not given so that men will marvel at the complexity of evil, but so that they will see that every evil power is temporary, judged, and doomed before Jehovah's decree. And it is not given to turn the people of God away from present obedience toward prophetic curiosity, but to teach them how to live now in the light of what God has promised to do.

For that reason, anyone who would understand the doctrine of last things must begin here. Before one asks about the antichrist, the great tribulation, the mark of the beast, the resurrection, the millennium, or the final judgment, one must understand what prophecy is. It is divine revelation, governed by the meaning intended by the inspired writer, given for the glory of Jehovah, centered in Jesus Christ, morally binding upon the hearer, and certain in its fulfillment. Only when prophecy is understood in that way can the rest of biblical eschatology be approached with clarity, seriousness, and hope.

CHAPTER 2 Explaining Signs of the End of the Age

The Meaning of the End of the Age

When Scripture speaks about the end of the age, it does not refer to the annihilation of the planet, the collapse of all divine purpose, or the extinction of mankind as such. It refers to the close of the present order of rebellion and the decisive transition into the next stage of God's kingdom administration. This distinction is essential, because many readers hear the language of "the end" and assume that the Bible is speaking only of total termination. But the prophets, Jesus, and the apostles speak of an ending that is also a beginning. The end of the present age means the end of lawless dominion in its current form, the end of unchecked deception, the end of beastly power as it now opposes God, and the end of the present arrangement under which death, corruption, and satanic rebellion continue. It also means the open manifestation of Christ's rule, the vindication of the faithful, and the advancement of God's purpose toward final restoration.

This is why the disciples' question in Matthew 24:3 must be read carefully. They ask, "What will be the sign of your presence and of the conclusion of the age?" Jesus does not rebuke the question as meaningless. He answers it at length because the end of the age is a real biblical category. His answer also shows that the end is not identified by one isolated event. It involves a pattern of developments that culminate in unparalleled tribulation, cosmic disturbance, and the visible coming of the Son of Man. The signs, therefore, are not random religious curiosities. They are part of a divinely ordered sequence that prepares the way for the public intervention of Christ in judgment and kingdom power.

The expression "age" itself points to a system, an order, a period of world-history under a particular moral and spiritual condition. The present age is marked by sin, deception, false religion, persecution, death, and rebellion against Jehovah. Even where the gospel advances, the world as a whole remains under hostile powers and under the influence of the wicked one. That is why Scripture can speak of "this age" as passing away and of a coming order under the reign of Christ. Jesus speaks of "this age" and "that coming one" in a way that distinguishes the present order from the future order of divine kingdom realization. Paul likewise contrasts "this present wicked age" with the redemptive purpose of God in Christ. The end of the age, then, is not a vague spiritual idea. It is the divinely appointed close of the present rebellious system of things.

Why Jesus Gave Signs of the End

Jesus did not give signs so that men could indulge speculation, build charts detached from the text, or claim private prophetic superiority. He gave signs so that His disciples would not be deceived, frightened, or spiritually unprepared. This purpose appears immediately in the Olivet Discourse. Before Jesus speaks of wars, famines, tribulation, or cosmic signs, He first says, "See that no one misleads you" (Matt. 24:4). The first concern is deception. That alone tells the reader how the signs are to be handled. They are not toys for the curious. They are safeguards for the faithful. Prophecy was given so that believers would remain steady when the appointed events begin to unfold.

This also explains why Jesus combines warning with restraint. He tells His disciples that certain things must happen, but He also refuses to allow premature conclusions. "You are going to hear of wars and reports of wars; see that you are not alarmed, for these things must take place, but the end is not yet" (Matt. 24:6). This statement is crucial. Not every upheaval is the end. Not every war, earthquake, famine, or social convulsion is the signal that the consummation has arrived. The signs must be read in the way Christ intended, not in the feverish way people often prefer. Some events belong to the general convulsions of the present age. Others mark the intensified approach of the end. The words of Jesus must govern the distinction.

Because of this, the signs are not given merely to identify chronology. They are given to form conduct. Jesus repeatedly moves from prophecy to exhortation. He says, "keep on the watch," "stay awake," and "prove yourselves ready" (Matt. 24:42, 44; 25:13). The signs are therefore morally charged. They summon the faithful to vigilance, endurance, and obedience. They teach that history is moving under divine decree toward a fixed conclusion, and that the right response is not panic or speculation, but covenant loyalty.

The First Sign: Deception and False Christs

The first sign Jesus gives is deception through false christs and false prophets. "Many will come on the basis of my name, saying, 'I am the Christ,' and will mislead many" (Matt. 24:5). Later He adds that many false prophets will arise and mislead many, and that false christs and false prophets will show great signs and wonders so as to mislead, if possible, even the chosen ones (Matt. 24:11, 24). This means the beginning of the end is not first marked by political chaos, but by religious deception. The assault on the truth comes before the visible consummation. This should not surprise any careful reader of Scripture, because the end-time conflict is always first theological before it becomes fully political and military.

This sign has broad significance. False christs are not merely political pretenders claiming messiahship in crude form. The antichristic principle works wherever the true identity, authority, and exclusiveness of Jesus Christ are denied, replaced, or counterfeited. A false christ can appear through outright denial, but also through doctrinal corruption, false worship, and spiritual systems that claim divine authority while departing from apostolic truth. That is why John says many antichrists had already arisen in the apostolic age and identifies antichrist by denial of the Son and refusal to confess Jesus Christ as having come in the flesh (1 John 2:18, 22-23; 4:2-3; 2 John 7). The signs of the end, therefore, must include the spread and intensification of theological falsehood.

Jesus' warning also shows that deception can be persuasive. He does not speak of flimsy error that can be dismissed without effort. He says false christs and false prophets will mislead many. Paul confirms the same danger when he says the man of lawlessness will come with all power and lying signs and wonders and with every unrighteous deception for those who are perishing (2 Thess. 2:9-10). The end of the age, then, is marked by intensified religious fraud, doctrinal corruption, and counterfeit claims to divine authority. The faithful must therefore judge all teaching by Scripture, not by emotional impact, public success, or apparent supernatural display.

Wars, Reports of Wars, and Global Unrest

After speaking of deception, Jesus says, "You are going to hear of wars and reports of wars" (Matt. 24:6). Luke adds tumults and disturbances among nations (Luke 21:9-10). Yet Jesus immediately adds, "see that you are not alarmed, for these things must take place, but the end is not yet." This is one of the most important controls on end-time interpretation. War by itself is not the final sign. The world has long been filled with conflict. The existence of battle, invasion, and upheaval does not by itself prove that the final consummation has arrived. Such events belong to the present age, and Christ calls them "the beginning of birth pangs" (Matt. 24:8).

The image of birth pangs is instructive. Birth pains are real, painful, and progressive. They indicate that something is moving toward a divinely appointed outcome. Yet the first pains are not the birth itself. In the same way, wars and global unrest indicate that the age is unstable and under judgment, but they are not themselves the final event. They belong to the pattern of escalating distress that characterizes the period leading toward the end. They show that the world order cannot secure peace, cannot heal itself, and cannot establish the kingdom of God through human effort.

This point also harmonizes with Daniel and Revelation. Daniel presents kingdoms as beastly powers arising from the turbulent sea of nations. The image itself suggests unrest, violence, and instability. Revelation likewise presents horsemen, judgments, and convulsions that belong to the period of conflict leading toward final intervention. The world is not moving toward self-generated peace. It is moving through upheaval toward the judgment of God and the appearing of Christ. Wars, then, are signs of a world under divine sentence, not signs that human dominion is finally maturing into righteousness.

Famines, Pestilences, and Earthquakes

Jesus next includes famines, pestilences, and earthquakes in various places (Matt. 24:7; Luke 21:11). These realities show that the instability of the age is not confined to politics. Creation itself groans under the burden of sin and divine judgment. Shortage, disease, natural upheaval, and fear all mark the condition of a world alienated from God. The signs of the end therefore extend beyond rulers and armies into the broader suffering of human life under the curse.

Yet here again, these are not signs to be isolated from the whole pattern. Famines alone do not prove that the great tribulation has begun. Earthquakes alone do not settle prophetic chronology. Jesus includes them as part of the beginning of birth pains. They belong to the age's instability, and their intensification contributes to the world's growing distress. Luke adds "fearful sights and great signs from heaven" (Luke 21:11), showing that the atmosphere of the end includes dread, foreboding, and the sense that creation itself is moving toward crisis.

These signs also carry a moral message. They show the fragility of human life and the inability of man to secure the future apart from God. Famines expose dependence. Pestilences expose mortality. Earthquakes expose the instability of what men assume is firm. The same world that boasts of progress and strength is repeatedly reminded that it does not control its own foundations. In this sense, these signs are humbling. They expose the weakness of the present order and point beyond man to the need for divine intervention.

Persecution, Betrayal, and Hatred

Jesus moves from general upheaval to direct hostility against His followers. "Then people will hand you over to tribulation and will kill you, and you will be hated by all the nations on account of my name" (Matt. 24:9). Luke expands this by speaking of arrests, betrayals by relatives and friends, and hatred because of Christ's name (Luke 21:12-17). This sign is especially important because it makes clear that the end of the age is not marked only by events in the world around believers. It is marked by direct pressure upon the faithful themselves.

Persecution belongs to the pattern of the end because the conflict is ultimately between the kingdom of God and the rebellious world. The closer history moves toward its appointed climax, the more clearly the line between faithfulness and hostility is drawn. Daniel already showed this in the little horn's war against the holy ones and in the arrogant rulers who exalt themselves against God. Jesus confirms it by warning His disciples that loyalty to Him will bring hatred. Revelation develops it further by showing the beast making war on the holy ones, the dragon persecuting the woman and the rest of her offspring, and the blood of the holy ones crying out under oppression (Rev. 6:9-11; 12:17; 13:7).

This persecution is not an accidental side effect of history. It is part of the appointed conflict. Yet Jesus does not present it as defeat. "The one who has endured to the end is the one who will be saved" (Matt. 24:13). Endurance, therefore, is itself a sign of genuine discipleship in the time of the end. The church is not told to conquer by worldly force, but by faithfulness under pressure. The faithful endure because Christ has overcome the world, because the kingdom belongs to Him, and because the sufferings of the present age do not nullify the certainty of the coming kingdom.

Apostasy and Lawlessness

Jesus then says, "Many will be stumbled and betray one another and hate one another," and "because of the increasing of lawlessness, the love of the greater number will grow cold" (Matt. 24:10, 12). This is a vital sign because it shows that the end is marked not only by external opposition but also by internal decay within the professing sphere. Apostasy, betrayal, and moral cooling are signs of the end of the age.

Paul makes the same point in 2 Thessalonians 2 when he says the apostasy must come first and the man of lawlessness be revealed. The end is therefore preceded by a great falling away from the truth. This is not merely the unbelief of the pagan world continuing as before. It is revolt within the sphere where truth had been known. It is the maturing of rebellion against divine revelation. The present age of profession without faith, religion without obedience, and doctrine without truth does not continue indefinitely. It moves toward a climactic exposure.

Lawlessness is especially important here. Lawlessness in Scripture is not simply social disorder. It is rebellion against the authority of God. The lawless one in 2 Thessalonians 2 represents concentrated, self-exalting apostasy in the sphere of worship. Jesus says lawlessness will increase and cause love to grow cold. That means the end of the age is not merely violent; it is morally disintegrating. People cast off restraint, truth is abandoned, and even those near the faith may harden into betrayal and hatred. These signs show a world and a professing religious sphere ripening for judgment.

The Good News of the Kingdom in All the Inhabited Earth

In the midst of warnings, Jesus gives a sign of hope and certainty: "This good news of the kingdom will be preached in all the inhabited earth for a witness to all the nations, and then the end will come" (Matt. 24:14). The end is not only marked by evil intensifying. It is also marked by the worldwide witness of the kingdom message. This is an essential balance. The signs of the end include not just darkness, but the continued advance of the gospel according to God's purpose.

The message being proclaimed is specifically "the good news of the kingdom." That matters. The gospel is not merely an offer of private comfort. It is the announcement of God's rule in Christ, the call to repentance and faith, and the declaration that the present order stands under sentence while the kingdom of God draws near. The witness goes to all nations, not necessarily meaning that every individual without exception hears, but that the kingdom message reaches the inhabited world as a divine testimony before the end comes.

This preaching is not presented as a human achievement that brings in the kingdom by gradual success. Rather, it is a witness given before the end. The nations hear, the world is confronted, and the kingdom is announced. The end then comes according to God's decree. Thus the preaching of the good news belongs to the signs of the end because it shows that history is moving under the command of Christ toward judgment and consummation. The nations are not left without testimony. The gospel confronts them before the final crisis arrives.

The Abomination of Desolation

A major turning point in Jesus' prophecy comes with the sign of "the abomination of desolation spoken of through Daniel the prophet" standing in the holy place (Matt. 24:15). This expression cannot be rightly understood apart from Daniel. Daniel speaks of profanation, desecration, arrogant power, and the setting up of something abominable in relation to the holy place and the end-time crisis (Dan. 9:27; 11:31; 12:11). Jesus deliberately directs readers back to Daniel because the pattern of the end has already been laid down there.

The abomination of desolation signifies an act or reality of extreme profanation connected with anti-God power and desecrating rebellion. It is not merely any offensive event. It is an end-time marker tied to the final concentrated crisis. Jesus says that when this occurs, those in Judea must flee immediately, because the unparalleled tribulation is at hand (Matt. 24:16-21). The sign, then, is not one of the general birth pangs. It belongs to the intensified final phase.

Because of its seriousness, the abomination cannot be reduced to symbolism without historical force. Daniel and Jesus both treat it as a real marker within the unfolding of the end. At the same time, it must be interpreted according to the scriptural pattern rather than forced into every passing event. The abomination belongs to the maturing anti-God order, to desecration in relation to what is holy, and to the final crisis preceding the appearing of Christ. It signals that lawless rebellion has reached a decisive and intolerable stage.

The Great Tribulation

Jesus then says, "For then there will be great tribulation such as has not occurred since the world's beginning until now, no, nor will occur again" (Matt. 24:21). This language echoes Daniel 12:1, which speaks of "a time of distress such as never occurred since there came to be a nation until that time." The connection is deliberate. Jesus is identifying the great tribulation as the Danielic unparalleled crisis of the time of the end.

This means the great tribulation is not simply the entire history of Christian suffering. Believers have always faced tribulation in the broad sense, and Jesus says in general that in the world His followers will have tribulation (John 16:33). But the great tribulation of Matthew 24 is a unique intensified period, not the whole age of suffering. Its uniqueness is stressed by the language "such as has not occurred ... nor will occur again." It marks the concentrated climax of conflict before Christ's visible return.

Jesus also says those days will be cut short for the sake of the chosen ones (Matt. 24:22). This means the tribulation, though severe, is measured by divine mercy. God does not surrender His people to endless destruction. The same God who reveals the tribulation also sets its limits. Revelation reflects this same theology. Evil powers rage, but only within limits. The beast is granted authority for an appointed time. The dragon persecutes, but he is not sovereign. The tribulation is terrible, yet governed by decree.

Cosmic Signs and the Coming of the Son of Man

After the tribulation, Jesus says the sun will be darkened, the moon will not give its light, the stars will fall from heaven, and the powers of the heavens will be shaken (Matt. 24:29). This is prophetic language drawn from the Old Testament, where cosmic disturbance accompanies divine judgment and world-shaking intervention. Isaiah uses such language for the judgment of Babylon (Isa. 13:10). Joel speaks of sun and moon darkening before the great and fear-inspiring day of Jehovah (Joel 2:30-31). Jesus now applies this kind of language to the climactic end-time intervention associated with His own coming.

These cosmic signs are not to be treated as decorative imagery with no referent. They signify a world-order shaken by divine intervention. The stable structures of the present rebellious age are thrown into convulsion because the King is about to appear. Then "the sign of the Son of Man" appears in heaven, and "all the tribes of the earth will beat themselves in grief, and they will see the Son of Man coming on the clouds of heaven with power and great glory" (Matt. 24:30). This language clearly echoes Daniel 7:13-14, where the Son of Man receives dominion, glory, and a kingdom.

The coming of the Son of Man is therefore the decisive answer to the signs of the end. The signs do not culminate in mere disaster. They culminate in the appearing of Christ. The world mourns because the age of rebellion is ending and because the One whom men have resisted is now revealed openly as Judge and King. At the same time, He sends out His angels with a great trumpet and gathers His chosen ones from the four winds (Matt. 24:31). This gathering is public, glorious, and connected directly with His visible coming. It is not a hidden event detached from the final manifestation. The signs of the end thus lead directly to the return of Christ, the gathering of His people, and the beginning of the next stage of kingdom rule.

The Significance of Israel, the Nations, and the Fig Tree

Jesus also uses the fig tree as a lesson: when its branch becomes tender and puts forth leaves, summer is near; in the same way, when the disciples see all these things, they know that He is near, at the doors (Matt. 24:32-33). The point of the fig tree is not speculative symbolism about a particular modern political entity. It is a lesson in discernment. Just as natural signs indicate a coming season, so the appointed prophetic signs indicate the nearness of the consummation.

This helps prevent two errors. One error ignores the signs and treats all prophecy as too obscure for practical understanding. The other error turns every event into a sign. Jesus teaches a middle way of sober discernment. The faithful are to recognize the pattern He gave. They are not to invent signs He did not give, nor are they to despise the signs He did give. The fig tree parable teaches that the signs have meaning and that the people of God are expected to perceive that meaning when the appointed sequence unfolds.

The nations also remain central in the signs of the end. Jesus speaks of all nations hating His followers, the good news being preached in all the inhabited earth, and all the tribes of the earth mourning at His coming. The end of the age is therefore global in scope. The conflict is not local only. The beastly order, the gospel witness, the tribulation, and the coming of Christ all unfold on a world scale. This corresponds to Daniel's universal kingdom vision and to Revelation's repeated references to peoples, tribes, tongues, and nations under the pressure of the final conflict.

Signs That Are Not Signs

A faithful doctrine of the signs of the end must also say what Jesus says is not yet the end. Wars by themselves are not the end. General upheaval is not yet the end. Fearful events alone are not the end. This is vital because people are often eager to identify the end in every crisis. Jesus forbids that impulse. He teaches His followers to distinguish between the beginning of birth pangs and the final, unparalleled tribulation. He teaches them to resist alarmism and remain watchful.

Likewise, not every religious movement, political tyrant, or natural disaster can be called the fulfillment of the final signs. Scripture itself distinguishes between the broad last-days pattern and the concentrated time of the end. There have long been many antichrists, yet there is still a climactic revelation of the man of lawlessness. There has long been tribulation, yet there is still the great tribulation. There have long been wars, yet there is still Armageddon. These distinctions matter because the Bible itself makes them. The faithful must not erase them by carelessness.

The Signs and the Call to Watchfulness

The signs of the end are not given to produce date-setting. Jesus says plainly that concerning that day and hour no one knows, neither the angels of the heavens nor the Son, but only the Father (Matt. 24:36). That means the signs do not grant men control over divine timing. They grant readiness, not mastery. The disciple is called to vigilance, not prophetic arrogance.

This is why Jesus compares His coming to the days of Noah. People ate, drank, married, and carried on ordinary life until the flood came and swept them all away (Matt. 24:37-39). The point is not that ordinary activities are sinful, but that the world continued in complacency until judgment overtook it. So it will be with the presence of the Son of Man. The signs prepare the faithful, but the unwatchful world remains exposed. Therefore, Jesus concludes with repeated exhortations to keep awake and remain ready.

The same message runs through the apostles. Paul says the day of Jehovah comes as a thief in the night, but believers are not in darkness that the day should overtake them as thieves, because they are sons of light and of day (1 Thess. 5:2-5). Peter says the day of the Lord will come as a thief, and therefore believers must live in holy conduct and godliness (2 Pet. 3:10-12). Revelation repeatedly says, "Happy is the one who stays awake" and calls the churches to conquer through faithfulness. Watchfulness is not nervous excitement. It is obedient readiness shaped by the certainty that Christ will come.

The Hope Within the Signs

Although the signs of the end include deception, violence, persecution, apostasy, and tribulation, they are not signs of defeat for the faithful. They are signs that the age of rebellion is nearing its appointed close. Jesus says that when the great heavenly disturbances begin, His followers should straighten up and lift their heads because their deliverance is drawing near (Luke 21:28). The same events that terrify the world bring hope to those who belong to Christ.

This is because the signs point beyond themselves. False christs point to the necessity of the true Christ. Tribulation points to the end of the present order. Lawlessness points to the coming destruction of the lawless one. The witness of the kingdom points to the certainty of divine rule. Cosmic shaking points to the removal of what can be shaken so that what cannot be shaken may remain. The mourning of the tribes points to the triumph of the Son of Man. In every case, the sign is not the destination. It is the marker on the road to Christ's appearing and the advancement of God's kingdom.

For that reason, the signs of the end must never be handled as though they were the center of prophecy. Christ is the center. The signs matter because they point to Him, warn concerning opposition to Him, and prepare the church for fidelity until He comes. When interpreted in that way, they do not create panic. They create seriousness, endurance, and hope.

Living in the Light of the End

To understand the signs of the end of the age is to understand how believers must live in the present. They must not be deceived by false religion or false christs. They must not be shaken by wars and tumults as though God had lost control. They must not be surprised by persecution, betrayal, or apostasy. They must remain faithful in proclaiming the good news of the kingdom. They must recognize that the present age is unstable and under sentence. They must interpret the growth of lawlessness and the rise of anti-God power in the light of Scripture, not according to worldly optimism. And they must fix their hope, not on the endurance of the present order, but on the appearing of the Son of Man.

This is the proper effect of the signs. They disentangle the heart from the world. They make obedience urgent. They teach discernment. They guard against both gullibility and alarmism. They expose the present age as temporary. Above all, they direct attention to Jesus Christ, whose coming ends the present rebellion and advances the kingdom of God into its next revealed stage.

The signs of the end, then, are real, scriptural, and meaningful. But they must be read in the order and proportion given by Christ. Deception comes first. General upheaval marks the beginning of birth pangs. Persecution, apostasy, and lawlessness intensify. The gospel witness continues. The abomination of desolation marks the transition into the final concentrated crisis. Great tribulation follows. Then come cosmic disturbance, the visible coming of the Son of Man, and the gathering of His chosen ones. This is the pattern Jesus gave. It stands in harmony with Daniel, with Paul's doctrine of the apostasy and the man of lawlessness, and with Revelation's unveiling of the final conflict.

Those who understand the signs rightly will not treat them as occasions for fear or pride. They will hear in them the voice of Christ calling for endurance, holiness, and hope. They will understand that the age is moving toward its appointed close, that Jehovah still rules over the kingdoms of men, and that the final word belongs not to the beastly order, but to the Lamb who will come with power and great glory.

CHAPTER 3 Explaining the Antichrist

The Only New Testament Writer Who Uses the Term Antichrist

Any careful study of the Antichrist must begin with a simple but decisive fact: the term antichrist appears only in the letters of John. It is not found in the Gospels, Acts, Paul's letters, Hebrews, James, Peter, Jude, or even in Revelation by that exact word. This fact matters greatly because it means that the doctrine of the Antichrist must first be defined where Scripture itself defines it. Many people begin with later religious tradition, popular end-time speculation, or a vague assumption that the Antichrist must be one future political tyrant. But the first duty of biblical interpretation is to let the inspired text establish its own categories. John must be allowed to define antichrist, just as Paul must be allowed to define the man of lawlessness, Daniel must be allowed to define the prophetic pattern of arrogant world power, and Revelation must be allowed to define the beastly order and its final rebellion.

John's first major statement appears in 1 John 2:18: "Young children, it is the last hour, and just as you have heard that antichrist is coming, even now many antichrists have arisen." That verse immediately corrects a shallow and popular error. Scripture does not teach that the whole doctrine of antichrist can be reduced to one isolated future figure and nothing more. John says that antichrist is coming, but he also says that many antichrists had already arisen in his own day. The biblical doctrine therefore includes both expectation and present reality. There is a coming antichristic culmination, but there is also an already-active antichristic presence operating in history. John does not choose between the singular and the plural. He joins them. The church must do the same.

This alone shows why the subject cannot be handled carelessly. If the church only looks for one future enemy, it may fail to recognize present enemies of the truth. John wrote so that believers would not make that mistake. The danger was already among them. It was not merely waiting in a distant century. The apostolic church itself faced many antichrists. That means the doctrine is not first about satisfying curiosity concerning future events. It is about discernment in the present. It is about recognizing when the truth concerning Jesus Christ is being opposed, denied, twisted, or replaced.

What the Word Antichrist Means

The word antichrist carries the sense of being against Christ and also standing in the place of Christ. It includes hostility and counterfeit. The antichristic spirit does not only attack openly from the outside. It also imitates, substitutes, and corrupts. This is why the doctrine is so serious. Crude unbelief is dangerous, but counterfeit Christianity is often more dangerous because it seeks to wear the appearance of truth while hollowing out its substance. Jesus warned of false christs and false prophets who would mislead many (Matt. 24:4-5, 11, 24). John's language fits directly into that wider warning. The antichristic reality opposes the true Christ by presenting false claims, false doctrine, false authority, and false worship.

This is why antichrist must be understood as theological before it is political. The deepest issue is not first state power, economic control, or military domination, though those realities may later become involved. The deepest issue is truth about Jesus Christ. Antichrist attacks the identity, person, authority, and saving work of the Son of God. That means a system may look religious, disciplined, intellectual, and morally serious, and still be antichristic if it denies the truth about Christ. The church must judge by apostolic doctrine, not outward impressiveness.

Many Antichrists Already at Work

John says, "even now many antichrists have arisen" (1 John 2:18). This means the church has lived with antichristic opposition from the apostolic age onward. Antichrist is not merely a final headline figure waiting at the end of history with no prior manifestation. The spirit and activity of antichrist were already present while the apostles were still alive. John adds, "From this we know that it is the last hour" (1 John 2:18). In other words, the presence of many antichrists was itself evidence that the church had entered the climactic epoch of redemptive history. The Messiah had come, the gospel had been proclaimed, and now the counterfeit reaction against Him was spreading.

John then explains one major feature of these antichrists: "They went out from us, but they were not of us" (1 John 2:19). This is profoundly important. The antichristic danger does not arise only from open paganism or unbelief outside the visible sphere of religion. It also arises from apostasy within the professing sphere. These were people who had once moved among believers, but they departed from apostolic truth. Their going out exposed what they truly were. John does not present them as merely confused. He presents them as evidence of antichristic rebellion.

This harmonizes with Paul's warning to the Ephesian elders that savage wolves would come in among the flock and that from among their own selves men would arise speaking twisted things to draw away disciples after themselves (Acts 20:29-30). It also fits Jesus' warning that false prophets would arise and mislead many. The church must never think that danger only comes from obvious outsiders. Some of the most serious threats arise where outward religious profession is closest to the truth while inward loyalty to Christ has already failed.

The Doctrinal Heart of the Antichrist

John defines the matter plainly in 1 John 2:22: "Who is the liar but the one who denies that Jesus is the Christ? This is the antichrist, the one who denies the Father and the Son." That statement is decisive. Antichrist is defined by christological denial. The Antichrist is not first identified by political charisma, military conquest, or economic manipulation. He is identified by falsehood concerning Jesus Christ. Whoever denies that Jesus is the Christ, the promised Messiah, stands in the lie that John calls antichrist.

John goes further. To deny the Son is also to deny the Father. "Everyone who denies the Son does not have the Father; the one who confesses the Son has the Father also" (1 John 2:23). This destroys the idea that people may reject the true identity of Jesus Christ while still maintaining a faithful relationship with God. Scripture gives no room for that claim. The Father has made Himself known through the Son. Jesus says, "He who has seen me has seen the Father" (John 14:9). He also says, "The one who does not honor the Son does not honor the Father who sent him" (John 5:23). Therefore, denial of the Son is not a minor doctrinal defect. It is rebellion against the revelation of God Himself.

The same point appears in 1 John 4:2-3: "By this you know the Spirit of God: every inspired expression that confesses Jesus Christ as having come in the flesh originates with God, but every inspired expression that does not confess Jesus does not originate with God. This is the antichrist's inspired expression." John again makes the issue doctrinal and spiritual. Antichrist is not merely bad behavior. It is a lying spirit, a false confession, and a theological revolt against the incarnation and identity of the Son of God. Second John 7 says the same thing: "Many deceivers have gone out into the world, those not confessing Jesus Christ as coming in the flesh. This is the deceiver and the antichrist." The church must therefore understand that the primary battlefield is truth about Christ.

The Spirit of Antichrist

John teaches not only that many antichrists have arisen, but also that the spirit of antichrist is already in the world. He says of the false confession, "This is the antichrist's inspired expression which you have heard was coming, and now it is already in the world" (1 John 4:3). This is a vital biblical category. Antichrist is not only a person-centered expectation. It is also a spiritual principle of opposition to Christ, active in doctrine, worship, and allegiance.

That means the church must learn to recognize antichristic patterns, not merely wait for a final label. Wherever the truth about Jesus Christ is denied, wherever His person is corrupted, wherever His authority is displaced, wherever another message claims spiritual legitimacy while rejecting apostolic truth, there the spirit of antichrist is already at work. This includes false religion, counterfeit Christian teaching, apostate systems, and movements that may use biblical language while denying the Son in substance.

This also explains why the doctrine of antichrist remains relevant in every age. John's words were not exhausted in the first century, because the antichristic spirit continues to oppose Christ until the final overthrow of evil. Yet his words were already true in the first century, which means believers must not postpone antichrist entirely into the future. The church lives in a world where antichristic rebellion is both present and moving toward fuller exposure.

The Relationship Between Antichrist and the Man of Lawlessness

The Antichrist must be distinguished from, though not separated from, Paul's teaching about the man of lawlessness in 2 Thessalonians 2:3-4. Paul writes that the day will not come unless the apostasy comes first and the man of lawlessness is revealed, the son of destruction, who opposes and exalts himself against every so-called god or object of worship, so that he sits in the temple of God, publicly showing himself to be a god. Paul does not use the word antichrist. John does. But the two doctrines clearly belong to the same broad conflict.

The man of lawlessness represents the concentrated expression of apostate rebellion in the sphere of worship. He is lawless because he rejects God's authority. He is self-exalting because he usurps divine place. He is tied to apostasy because his revelation is preceded by large-scale departure from the truth. This harmonizes deeply with John's teaching that antichrist arises through doctrinal denial and departure from apostolic truth. Yet the terms should not be carelessly flattened into exact synonyms. John defines antichrist by christological denial and many present deceivers. Paul defines the man of lawlessness by apostate self-exaltation and final exposure. The relationship is one of theological unity without careless collapse of categories.

Paul also says, "the mystery of lawlessness is already at work" (2 Thess. 2:7). That language parallels John's claim that the spirit of antichrist is already in the world. What is later revealed in concentrated form is already operative in seed, principle, and hidden activity. This means antichristic and lawless rebellion develop historically before reaching final maturity. The end does not appear out of nowhere. The final crisis grows out of forces already active.

The Relationship Between Antichrist and the Beast

Revelation presents the beast from the sea, the beast from the earth, the image of the beast, the mark of the beast, and Babylon the Great. These realities belong to the final anti-God order, but the book does not use the specific word antichrist for them. Once again, careful distinctions are necessary. The beast is not simply a careless synonym for antichrist, though the beastly order is plainly antichristic. The beast represents mature anti-God political power energized by the dragon. The second beast or false prophet gives religious support to the first beast, performing deceptive signs and directing worship toward the beastly system (Rev. 13:11-15). In this sense Revelation shows the fully developed political-religious structure of rebellion.

This connects closely to antichrist because the final conflict is always against the true Christ. The beast blasphemes God, persecutes the holy ones, and wages war against the Lamb (Rev. 13:6-7; 17:14). The false prophet supports false worship. The mark of the beast signifies allegiance. Babylon intoxicates the nations with corruption and false religion. All of this belongs to one broad anti-Christ system. Yet again, Scripture is more precise than popular language often is. John's antichrist language, Paul's man of lawlessness language, and Revelation's beast language should be read together without erasing their distinctions. Together they show doctrinal denial, apostate self-exaltation, and mature beastly world-order rebellion.

Is the Antichrist One Person or Many?

Scripture requires a balanced answer. John clearly says many antichrists have arisen. Therefore the doctrine cannot be reduced to one person only. At the same time, he also says, "you have heard that antichrist is coming" (1 John 2:18). This leaves room for a recognized climactic expression of antichristic rebellion. The biblical picture, therefore, is not either many or one, but many moving toward fuller concentration.

This pattern fits the wider biblical witness. There are many deceivers, yet also a final lawless revelation. There are many false prophets, yet also a climactic false prophet. There is long-standing beastly dominion in history, yet also a mature final beastly order. The church should therefore reject both extremes. It should not ignore the many antichrists already active in history, and it should not deny the possibility of a final intensified expression of antichristic rebellion. Scripture teaches both diffusion and culmination.

This also protects believers from naïve futurism. If antichrist is only future, then current doctrinal corruption may be treated too lightly. But if antichrist is only a broad principle with no final concentration, then Scripture's warnings about the mature anti-God order are dulled. The right view keeps both truths together: many antichrists now, final exposure still ahead.

The Antichrist and False Worship

The conflict surrounding the Antichrist is at heart a conflict over worship. John defines antichrist doctrinally, but Scripture as a whole shows that doctrine and worship cannot be separated. False teaching about Christ leads to false worship. Paul's man of lawlessness exalts himself in the realm of worship. Revelation's beast demands worship. The false prophet directs the world toward worship of the beast. Babylon intoxicates nations into idolatrous participation. Therefore, the Antichrist must not be understood merely as an intellectual error. The doctrine corrupts worship, loyalty, and the conscience.

This explains why the mark of the beast is so serious. It is not first about technology or commerce in the shallow sense. It is about allegiance. Buying and selling become instruments within a larger demand for loyalty to an anti-God order, but the heart of the issue remains worship. Likewise, antichristic doctrine is not a harmless alternative perspective. It is a rival claim upon the soul. It demands that men reject the true Christ in favor of a substitute. This is why John treats denial of the Son as so severe. It is not simply inaccurate theology. It is idolatrous rebellion.

The Antichrist and the Last Hour

John's statement, "it is the last hour" (1 John 2:18), shows that antichrist belongs to the final epoch of redemptive history. The church has lived in the last days since the exaltation of Christ, and in that broad sense it has also lived with antichristic opposition from the beginning. Yet the last hour language also creates urgency. The antichristic presence is not a distant, irrelevant matter. It is a pressing reality in the church age, intensifying as history moves toward its appointed climax.

This means believers must always combine vigilance with patience. Vigilance is necessary because the spirit of antichrist is already in the world. Patience is necessary because not every manifestation of antichristic rebellion is yet the final exposure. The church must live between present discernment and future expectation. It must test the spirits now, resist doctrinal corruption now, reject false christs now, and also understand that a fuller crisis still lies ahead.

How Believers Must Respond

The biblical response to the Antichrist is not fear, obsession, or reckless speculation. It is fidelity to the apostolic truth concerning Jesus Christ. John repeatedly gives this response. Believers are to remain in what they heard from the beginning (1 John 2:24). They are to test the spirits (1 John 4:1). They are to confess the Son truly. They are to reject deceivers who do not remain in the teaching of Christ (2 John 9-11). The first defense against the Antichrist is doctrinal steadfastness.

Jesus also warns believers not to be misled by claims of hidden or secret appearances. "If they say to you, 'Look! He is in the wilderness,' do not go out; 'Look! He is in the inner rooms,' do not believe it" (Matt. 24:26). The true coming of Christ will not require esoteric knowledge or secret circles. It will be public, glorious, and unmistakable, like lightning flashing from east to west (Matt. 24:27). The church must therefore reject every movement that claims special access to a hidden christ, a secret appearance, or a private revelation that displaces the public testimony of Scripture.

Paul adds another essential response: love of the truth. Those deceived by the lawless one perish because they did not accept the love of the truth so that they might be saved (2 Thess. 2:10). This is decisive. Protection from antichristic deception is not found merely in curiosity about prophecy. It is found in loving the truth. Those who do not love the truth are vulnerable to the lie, no matter how religious they appear. Those who love the truth, by contrast, are guarded by God through the Word He has given.

The Destruction of the Antichristic Order

The final word about the Antichrist is not his rise, but his destruction. Paul says the lawless one will be brought to nothing by the manifestation of Christ's presence (2 Thess. 2:8). Revelation says the beast and the false prophet are captured and thrown into the lake of fire (Rev. 19:20). The kings of the earth gather against the Lamb, but the Lamb conquers them because He is Lord of lords and King of kings (Rev. 17:14). The dragon himself is finally judged, and all evil is removed from God's creation.

This is why the doctrine of the Antichrist must never become the center of Christian attention. Scripture reveals antichristic rebellion so that the church may discern it, resist it, and endure through it. But the center remains Christ. The church does not await the Antichrist in dread as though evil controls the future. It awaits Jesus Christ, who will destroy the lawless and beastly order at His appearing. The Antichrist is temporary. Christ is everlasting. The spirit of antichrist works now, but the Spirit-inspired truth of God remains greater. "The One who is in you is greater than the one who is in the world" (1 John 4:4).

The Antichrist in the Light of Christ's Victory

When the doctrine is understood biblically, several truths stand firm. The Antichrist is real, but the doctrine begins with John's own definition, not with later speculation. Antichrist is first a matter of denying Jesus as the Christ, denying the Father and the Son, and refusing the truth of the incarnation. Many antichrists were already active in the apostolic age, proving that the church must always be on guard against present deception. Yet Scripture also leaves room for a final, more concentrated antichristic expression in relation to the apostasy, the man of lawlessness, and the beastly political-religious order.

The conflict is doctrinal, spiritual, and doxological. It concerns truth, worship, and allegiance. The false christ must be rejected because only the true Christ is Lord. The false prophet must be rejected because only God's Word is truth. The beastly order must be rejected because only Jehovah and the Lamb are worthy of worship. And the church must remain in the teaching heard from the beginning, loving the truth, testing the spirits, and enduring with confidence until Christ appears.

The final certainty is not the power of antichristic rebellion, but the triumph of Jesus Christ. The Antichrist opposes, but Christ reigns. The lawless one exalts himself, but Christ will destroy him. The beast gathers the nations, but the Lamb conquers. The present age may be filled with deception, betrayal, and counterfeit worship, but it is moving toward a fixed end. The true Christ will appear, every rival will fall, and the kingdom will belong openly to God and to His Christ. That is why the doctrine of the Antichrist, rightly understood, does not leave the faithful in fear. It leaves them in vigilance, in truth, and in hope.

CHAPTER 4 Explaining the Man of Lawlessness

The Setting of the Doctrine

The doctrine of the man of lawlessness is found most directly in 2 Thessalonians 2:1-12. It is one of the clearest passages in the New Testament concerning the final apostasy and the concentrated expression of anti-God rebellion before the visible return of Jesus Christ. Yet it has often suffered from confusion because readers either isolate it from the rest of biblical prophecy or merge it carelessly with every other hostile figure in Scripture. The right approach is to begin where Paul begins, follow his argument closely, and then place his teaching alongside the wider prophetic framework already established in Daniel, in the words of Jesus, and in Revelation. Paul is not writing fantasy, and he is not satisfying curiosity. He is correcting alarm, exposing deception, and anchoring believers in revealed truth.

The Thessalonian believers had become troubled by claims that the day of the Lord had already come or was immediately present in a way that unsettled them. Paul writes, "Now we request you, brothers, with regard to the presence of our Lord Jesus Christ and our being gathered together to Him, that you not be quickly shaken from your reason or be disturbed either by a spirit or by a message or by a letter as though from us, to the effect that the day of the Lord has come" (2 Thess. 2:1-2). This opening is essential. The doctrine of the man of lawlessness is not presented as an isolated end-time curiosity. It is given in direct connection with two realities: the presence of Christ and the gathering of believers to Him. Paul is therefore dealing with the same broad prophetic horizon Jesus addressed in the Olivet Discourse and the same public event that includes the appearing of Christ, the defeat of evil, and the vindication of the faithful.

This means the doctrine cannot be used to support a secret or hidden coming of Christ detached from the destruction of the lawless one. Paul explicitly ties the gathering of believers to the same eschatological setting in which the man of lawlessness is revealed and later destroyed. The flow of the chapter is plain. Believers are not to think the day has already arrived because certain things must occur first. There must be the apostasy, and there must be the revealing of the man of lawlessness. Then, in God's appointed order, Christ appears and destroys him. The passage does not divide Christ's coming into disconnected phases. It presents one coherent sequence governed by divine decree.

Paul's Warning Against Premature Claims

Paul's first pastoral burden is to guard the church against premature prophetic excitement. "Let no one deceive you in any way," he says, "because it will not come unless the apostasy comes first, and the man of lawlessness is revealed, the son of destruction" (2 Thess. 2:3). This is the controlling statement of the passage. The day of the Lord cannot be said to have arrived while the apostasy and the revealing of the lawless one remain unfulfilled. Paul's concern is not merely accuracy in a narrow prophetic sense. It is stability. False claims about the nearness or arrival of the day were shaking believers.

Prophetic error produces spiritual instability. Therefore, prophetic truth must be stated clearly.

The warning against deception also places the doctrine of the man of lawlessness within a wider pattern of end-time falsehood. Jesus had already warned that many false prophets would arise and mislead many, and that false christs and false prophets would show great signs and wonders to mislead, if possible, even the chosen ones (Matt. 24:11, 24). Paul's concern is of the same kind. The church must not be carried away by excitement, fear, or claims clothed in spiritual language. Truth about the future must be governed by what God has actually revealed, not by reports, experiences, or messages that appear impressive.

This also means that the doctrine of the man of lawlessness belongs to the church's defense against deception. It is not given so that believers may become obsessed with identifying personalities before their time. It is given so they will know that the final rebellion has an appointed sequence. The presence of error, the rise of apostasy, and the revelation of the lawless one all belong within that sequence. The church must therefore remain anchored in apostolic teaching and not be driven about by every prophetic claim.

The Meaning of the Apostasy

Paul says the day will not come unless "the apostasy comes first" (2 Thess. 2:3). The word translated apostasy denotes rebellion, falling away, or revolt. In context, it cannot be reduced to general wickedness in society. The world has always been wicked. Nor can it be reduced to ordinary unbelief among the nations. Paul is speaking of a rebellion tied to the sphere of revealed truth and to the religious setting in which the man of lawlessness operates. The apostasy is therefore a falling away from the truth, not merely a continuation of pagan ignorance.

This fits the wider New Testament pattern. Jesus warned that many would be stumbled and betray one another, and that because of increasing lawlessness the love of the greater number would grow cold (Matt. 24:10-12). Paul tells Timothy that in later times some will fall away from the faith, paying attention to deceitful spirits and teachings of demons (1 Tim. 4:1). He warns that evil men and impostors will proceed from bad to worse, misleading and being misled (2 Tim. 3:13). Peter speaks of false teachers secretly introducing destructive sects, even denying the Master who bought them (2 Pet. 2:1). Jude describes ungodly men who have crept in unnoticed and turn the grace of God into brazen conduct while denying Jesus Christ (Jude 4). The apostasy of 2 Thessalonians 2 belongs to this same line of revealed truth being abandoned from within the professing sphere.

That point is crucial because it prevents a shallow reading of the passage. The man of lawlessness does not arise in a religious vacuum. He is linked to revolt in the sphere of truth and worship. This is why the final rebellion is so serious. It is not only political opposition from the outside. It is also apostate corruption from within the professing world. The church must therefore understand that one of the chief signs before the day of the Lord is not merely increasing public immorality, but religious defection, doctrinal collapse, and the maturing of rebellion where truth had once been confessed.

The Identity of the Man of Lawlessness

Paul identifies the figure as "the man of lawlessness" and "the son of destruction" (2 Thess. 2:3). These designations are rich with meaning. He is a man of lawlessness because he embodies rebellion against God's order, authority, and truth. Lawlessness in Scripture is not merely social chaos. It is disregard for God's will. Jesus says that at the conclusion of the age the Son of Man will gather out of His kingdom all causes for stumbling and those practicing lawlessness (Matt. 13:41). He warns that many will say "Lord, Lord," but will be rejected as workers of lawlessness (Matt. 7:23). Lawlessness therefore includes religious profession without submission to God. It is rebellion under a spiritual appearance. That fits Paul's portrait perfectly.

He is also the "son of destruction." This expression identifies both character and destiny. As "son of destruction," he belongs to ruin, bears the character of ruin, and moves toward divinely appointed destruction. The same kind of expression is used of Judas in John 17:12, not to say merely that Judas would perish, but that he stood in a peculiar relation to destruction by his character and betrayal. The lawless one likewise is marked out as a figure of concentrated rebellion destined for decisive judgment. Paul therefore names him in a way that already anticipates his end. No matter how exalted he appears, destruction belongs to him.

The phrase "man of lawlessness" also suggests concentration and embodiment. Paul is not simply speaking of abstract lawlessness. He is speaking of lawlessness brought to a head, made visible, and publicly revealed in a concentrated expression. This fits the broader biblical pattern whereby long-developing evil reaches a mature form. There are many antichrists, but antichristic rebellion can also come to concentrated manifestation. The mystery of lawlessness is already at work, yet the lawless one will be revealed. Beastly empire has many historical expressions, yet Revelation unveils a mature final beastly order. Scripture therefore often presents both broad principle and concentrated culmination. The man of lawlessness belongs to that pattern.

His Self-Exaltation in the Sphere of Worship

Paul describes the lawless one as "the one who opposes and exalts himself above every so-called god or object of worship, so that he sits in the temple of God, publicly showing himself to be a god" (2 Thess. 2:4). This statement is one of the most solemn in the entire passage because it reveals the heart of the rebellion. The lawless one is not content with immorality or unbelief in a broad sense. He exalts himself in the sphere of worship. He is an opposer, a rival claimant, and a usurper of divine place.

The language here echoes Daniel. Daniel 7 describes the little horn speaking great things against the Most High and wearing down the holy ones (Dan. 7:25). Daniel 8 portrays a fierce king who exalts himself and magnifies himself even against the Prince of the host (Dan. 8:11, 25). Daniel 11 speaks of a king who exalts and magnifies himself above every god and speaks monstrous things against the God of gods (Dan. 11:36). Paul stands in continuity with that prophetic pattern. The lawless one belongs to the line of arrogant self-exalting power opposed to Jehovah and to His people. He is not an isolated invention of Paul's thought. He is the New Testament concentration of a prophetic pattern already disclosed in Daniel.

His sitting "in the temple of God" has been interpreted in various ways, but several points are clear from the language Paul uses. First, the setting is religious, not merely civil. Paul is not describing a military occupation alone. He is describing usurpation in the sphere that belongs to God. Second, the action is public. He "publicly shows himself" to be a god. The issue is open claim, not hidden influence only. Third, the essence of the act is self-deification. Whether by direct divine claim, assumed ultimate authority, or the demand for worshipful allegiance, the lawless one seeks the place that belongs to God alone.

The temple language must be read in harmony with the broader New Testament use of temple terminology. Paul can speak of the church corporately as God's temple (1 Cor. 3:16-17; Eph. 2:21), and he can also use temple language more broadly for the sphere of worship and divine claim. In this context, the main point is not architectural detail but religious usurpation. The lawless one rises within the realm that pertains to God, presenting himself in a way that belongs only to deity. This is why the apostasy must precede him. His revelation belongs within a setting of religious corruption, revolt, and counterfeit worship.

Paul's Reminder of Prior Teaching

Paul says, "Do you not remember that while I was still with you, I was telling you these things?" (2 Thess. 2:5). This statement matters because it shows that the doctrine of the man of lawlessness was not a novelty introduced in panic. It belonged to apostolic instruction from the beginning. The Thessalonians had already been taught a framework of end-time events. Paul is now reminding them of truths they should already know.

This also demonstrates that prophecy had a pastoral place in apostolic teaching. Paul did not consider eschatology a fringe subject. He regarded it as necessary for the church's stability and hope. The same is true throughout the New Testament. Jesus taught His disciples at length concerning the end of the age. Paul wrote of the resurrection, the coming of Christ, the day of the Lord, the apostasy, and the lawless one. Peter wrote about the day of God and the dissolution of the present heavens and earth. John received Revelation for the churches.

The doctrine of last things is therefore not peripheral. It directly affects how believers endure, worship, and resist deception.

The Restrainer and the Present Holding Back

Paul next says, "And you know what restrains him now, so that he will be revealed in his own time. For the mystery of lawlessness is already at work; only there is one who restrains now until he is out of the way" (2 Thess. 2:6-7). These verses have long been difficult, but the broad meaning is clear even where every detail is not. The lawless one is not revealed simply because evil wishes it. He is held back until God's appointed time. There is restraint in operation, and there is also a hidden working of lawlessness already underway.

The expression "mystery of lawlessness" is especially significant. A mystery in Scripture is not an unsolvable puzzle. It is a reality once hidden and now disclosed by God. Here the mystery of lawlessness refers to the concealed but active development of rebellion before its full exposure. Paul's point is that the final lawless manifestation does not appear out of nowhere. The principle is already working. The rebellion is already fermenting. The apostasy is already developing. What later becomes public is already moving beneath the surface.

This parallels John's teaching about the spirit of antichrist. John says the antichristic spirit was already in the world in his own day (1 John 4:3). Paul says the mystery of lawlessness is already at work. Both apostles therefore teach that the final anti-God climax has present roots. The church must not imagine that the end will arrive without prior spiritual corruption. The seeds are already active wherever truth is denied, worship is corrupted, and self-exalting rebellion advances.

At the same time, Paul emphasizes restraint. The lawless one is revealed "in his own time." This phrase places the whole matter under divine appointment. Evil is active, but it is not sovereign. Even the final lawless manifestation cannot appear before the time appointed by God. Restraint, whatever its precise mode, functions under divine decree. The Most High remains the ruler over history. This is completely consistent with Daniel's measured times and appointed ends and with Revelation's repeated statements that beastly power is "given" authority for only a set period.

Because Paul says the Thessalonians knew what or who restrains, it is likely he had given them fuller oral teaching not preserved in the letter. For that reason, interpreters must exercise humility. The passage teaches restraint clearly, but it does not authorize reckless certainty beyond what Paul states. The church can affirm that God, in His providential order, prevents the lawless climax until the appointed time. It can also affirm that the removal of restraint is part of the divinely governed sequence. But the exact mechanism should not be turned into dogma where the text itself remains measured.

The Revelation and Destruction of the Lawless One

Paul then says, "And then that lawless one will be revealed, whom the Lord Jesus will do away with by the spirit of His mouth and bring to nothing by the manifestation of His presence" (2 Thess. 2:8). This verse is decisive for the entire doctrine. The lawless one is revealed, but his revelation is temporary and his doom certain. His end comes by the visible intervention of Christ.

Two features stand out. First, the destruction is linked directly to "the manifestation of His presence." This means the downfall of the lawless one occurs at Christ's open appearing, not at a hidden preliminary event detached from public judgment. Paul's language harmonizes with Matthew 24, where the Son of Man appears in glory after the tribulation, and with Revelation 19, where the rider on the white horse judges and destroys the beastly order. The lawless one does not survive into some later phase after Christ's public coming. He is overthrown by it.

Second, Paul uses language drawn from Isaiah 11:4, where the Messianic ruler strikes the earth with the rod of His mouth and slays the wicked with the breath of His lips. Paul therefore places Jesus Christ in the role of the promised Davidic ruler who judges by divine authority. The spirit or breath of His mouth signifies sovereign, effortless judgment by His spoken authority. The one who exalted himself in the realm of worship is destroyed by the true Lord whose word cannot fail.

This is of great importance pastorally. However terrifying the lawless one appears, Scripture never treats him as a rival equal to Christ. He is revealed only at the appointed time, allowed to function only within measured bounds, and destroyed the moment Christ manifests His presence in glory. The church must therefore never view the man of lawlessness in isolation from the supremacy of Jesus Christ. The doctrine is given not to magnify evil, but to expose its temporary and doomed character.

Lying Signs and Unrighteous Deception

Paul continues: "that one's presence is according to the working of Satan with all power and signs and lying wonders, and with every unrighteous deception for those who are perishing" (2 Thess. 2:9-10). This reveals the satanic energy behind the lawless one. His coming or presence is not merely human charisma. It operates "according to the working of Satan." The final rebellion is therefore not explained fully at the sociological or political level. It is satanically energized opposition to God.

The lawless one comes with "all power and signs and lying wonders." These expressions do not necessarily mean that every display is unreal in the sense of being fake. Rather, they are lying in their purpose and effect. They serve falsehood. They confirm deception. They support rebellion against the truth. This harmonizes again with Jesus' warning that false christs and false prophets would show great signs and wonders so as to mislead (Matt. 24:24). The end-time conflict includes counterfeit supernatural display. Therefore the church must not judge truth by power alone. The issue is always whether the sign confirms God's Word or contradicts it.

Paul says this deception is "for those who are perishing, because they did not accept the love of the truth so as to be saved" (2 Thess. 2:10). Here the moral reason for deception is stated plainly. Men are not lost because they lacked data only. They are lost because they rejected the truth. The phrase "love of the truth" is strong. It does not refer merely to intellectual agreement. It refers to loyal embrace of the truth God has revealed. Those who refuse that love become vulnerable to the lie. This is why doctrinal indifference is so dangerous. The final deception does not overtake only the openly irreligious. It overtakes those who refuse the truth while remaining exposed to religious claims.

Paul adds that God sends upon them a working of error so that they may believe the lie, in order that all may be judged who did not believe the truth but took pleasure in unrighteousness (2 Thess. 2:11-12). This is judicial language. God does not become the author of falsehood. Rather, He gives over the truth-rejecting to the deception they have chosen. The same principle appears elsewhere in Scripture. Pharaoh hardens his heart, and God also hardens Pharaoh in judgment. Men exchange the truth of God for a lie, and God gives them over to degrading passions and a disapproved mind (Rom. 1:24-28). In the same way, those who reject the truth and delight in unrighteousness are judicially abandoned to the deception of the lawless one.

This makes the doctrine intensely serious. The man of lawlessness is not merely a subject for theological discussion. He is part of God's judgment upon truth-rejecting rebellion. The church's safety, therefore, lies not in speculation but in steadfast love for the truth.

The Temple of God and the Sphere of Apostasy

Because Paul says the lawless one sits in the temple of God, the question arises as to the sphere in which this rebellion unfolds. The strongest emphasis in the passage is that the lawless one operates in relation to worship and religious claim. He is not merely a secular tyrant with no connection to sacred things. His self-exaltation takes place where God's name is professed and where divine honor is claimed.

This strongly supports the conclusion that the final rebellion has an apostate religious character. It is anti-God, but not in the form of simple irreligion alone. It is counterfeit worship, usurpation, and false claim within the realm that pertains to God. This fits perfectly with the apostasy that must come first. The lawless one stands not merely against an empty background of unbelief, but against a history of religious corruption, defection, and counterfeit profession. The great danger is therefore not only from hostile nations, but from falsehood that arises close to holy things.

This is one reason the doctrine of the man of lawlessness must never be isolated from the doctrine of antichrist. John shows many antichrists arising from within the professing sphere. Paul shows the man of lawlessness exalting himself in the sphere of worship after the apostasy. Both apostles warn against rebellion growing near the truth before it reaches full exposure.

The Man of Lawlessness in Relation to Daniel and Revelation

Paul's lawless one should be read in continuity with Daniel's arrogant rulers and Revelation's beastly order. Daniel presents kings who magnify themselves, persecute the holy ones, profane the sanctuary, and oppose the God of heaven. Daniel 7, 8, and 11 all contribute elements of this pattern. Revelation then shows the mature final form of anti-God political-religious power in the beast, the false prophet, and Babylon the Great. The beast blasphemes God, persecutes the holy ones, and receives worship. The false prophet performs deceptive signs to direct men toward beast-worship. The whole structure is anti-God and anti-Christ.

Paul's lawless one belongs within this prophetic framework. He is not every aspect of it, but he fits within it as concentrated apostate self-exaltation in the sphere of worship. This is why the passage must not be detached from the wider biblical canon. Daniel lays the pattern. Jesus warns of the final crisis. Paul explains the apostasy and lawless revelation. Revelation unveils the mature beastly order and its destruction. Taken together, these passages form a consistent picture rather than disconnected predictions.

The Church's Duty in Light of This Doctrine

After describing the deception and judgment surrounding the lawless one, Paul turns to assurance and exhortation. He gives thanks because God chose believers from the beginning for salvation through sanctification by the Spirit and faith in the truth (2 Thess. 2:13). He then commands them to stand firm and hold to the traditions taught by the apostles (2 Thess. 2:15). This is the pastoral heart of the chapter. The doctrine of the man of lawlessness is not intended to leave believers terrified. It is intended to drive them into deeper steadfastness.

The proper response is to stand firm in apostolic truth. The final deception overtakes those who do not love the truth. Therefore the church must cling to the truth. The apostasy is a falling away from revealed doctrine. Therefore the church must remain in it. The lawless one exalts himself in the sphere of worship. Therefore the church must render worship only to God through Jesus Christ. The final conflict is over truth and worship, and believers must be rooted where God has spoken.

This also means the church must reject every form of prophetic sensationalism that distracts from obedience. Paul does not urge the Thessalonians to speculate endlessly about the restrainer or to identify every public figure as the lawless one. He urges them not to be deceived, to hold fast to the truth, and to be comforted by God's calling and purpose. Eschatology is not meant to produce instability. It is meant to produce endurance.

The Certain Triumph of Christ

The doctrine of the man of lawlessness reaches its proper conclusion only when it is read in the light of Christ's victory. The lawless one comes with satanic energy, deceptive signs, and arrogant self-exaltation. He belongs to the final apostasy and stands in the sphere of worship as a rival claimant. Yet his end is settled before his full revelation even begins. He is the son of destruction. He is restrained until the appointed time. He is revealed only to be destroyed by the manifestation of Christ's presence.

This is the comfort of the passage. Evil may mature, deception may intensify, and apostasy may spread, but none of these things alter the supremacy of Jesus Christ. The church must know what lies ahead, but it must know even more certainly who rules ahead. The Lord Jesus does not struggle to overcome the lawless one. He brings him to nothing by His appearing. The same Christ who died, rose, and now reigns will openly manifest His authority, and every false claimant in the sphere of worship will collapse before Him.

Therefore the doctrine of the man of lawlessness is not ultimately a doctrine about the strength of rebellion. It is a doctrine about the certainty of Christ's judgment upon rebellion. It warns of apostasy so the church will not be surprised. It reveals deception so the church will love the truth. It unveils the lawless one so the church will not confuse false worship with the kingdom of God. And it sets all of this within the context of the Lord's coming so that the faithful may endure with confidence. The present age may move toward concentrated rebellion, but it is moving also toward the visible triumph of the Son of God, who alone is worthy of worship and whose kingdom cannot be shaken.

CHAPTER 5 Explaining the Mark of the Beast – 666

The Place of the Mark Within Biblical Prophecy

The mark of the beast is one of the most discussed and most misunderstood subjects in biblical prophecy. Many readers approach it with fear, speculation, or shallow certainty. Some reduce it to a single technological device. Others treat it as if it were only a vague spiritual metaphor without concrete consequences. Neither approach does justice to the text. The mark of the beast appears in Revelation 13 and must be interpreted in the immediate context of the dragon, the beast from the sea, the beast from the earth, false worship, coercive allegiance, and the final conflict between God and the rebellious world order. The mark is not an isolated curiosity. It belongs to a whole anti-God system of power, worship, and identification.

Revelation 13 presents two beasts. The first beast rises from the sea, receives power and authority from the dragon, blasphemes God, and wages war against the holy ones (Rev. 13:1-7). The second beast rises from the earth, performs deceptive signs, directs the earth's inhabitants to worship the first beast, and enforces a visible system of allegiance (Rev. 13:11-17). The mark belongs to this second beast's activity. It is therefore tied directly to religious deception and beast-worship. The passage itself does not allow the mark to be studied apart from worship. This is the first major safeguard in interpretation. The mark is not first about commerce, technology, or state administration. It is first about worshipful loyalty to the anti-God order.

This means the mark of the beast should never be approached as though the Bible were merely offering a puzzle about future economic control. Revelation is showing the maturing of a beastly world order that seeks to claim human beings the way God claims His own servants. The dragon gives authority to the beast. The beast demands worship. The second beast enforces that worship. The mark then functions as a visible sign of belonging, allegiance, and participation within that rebellious structure. The issue at the center is always this: Who has the right to command the conscience, direct the life, and receive the worship of mankind? Revelation's answer is uncompromising. Worship belongs only to God and to the Lamb. The mark of the beast is the counterfeit sign of a rival claim.

The Literary Context of Revelation 13

Revelation 13 cannot be interpreted responsibly if it is detached from the chapters around it. Revelation 12 shows the dragon, identified as the Devil and Satan, cast down and enraged against the woman and the rest of her offspring, those who observe the commandments of God and hold to the testimony of Jesus (Rev. 12:9, 17). Revelation 13 then shows how the dragon acts in history through beastly powers. The sea beast embodies anti-God dominion in political and imperial form. The earth beast, later called the false prophet, functions in a religious and propagandistic role, supporting the first beast and directing humanity into false worship (Rev. 16:13; 19:20;

20:10). The mark is therefore not a random invention. It is the visible sign attached to the dragon's delegated earthly order.

This context already shows that the mark is not neutral. It belongs to satanically energized rebellion. The dragon is not presented as an equal rival to God, but as a rebel acting within divinely limited permission. The beast is not a random symbol for any disliked government, but a concentrated anti-God power arising in continuity with Daniel's vision of beastly dominion. Daniel 7 presents successive empires as beasts rising from the sea, and Revelation takes up that imagery to describe the final matured expression of rebellious world power. This means the mark also belongs to that prophetic line. It is a sign attached to the climax of beastly empire, not a symbol to be assigned carelessly to every feared development in history.

The literary flow also shows that the mark stands in contrast to God's own sealing of His people. In Revelation 7, the servants of God are sealed on their foreheads. In Revelation 14, the Lamb stands on Mount Zion with the one hundred forty-four thousand who have His name and His Father's name written on their foreheads (Rev. 14:1). Revelation therefore establishes two opposing marks of ownership and allegiance. God marks His own, and the beast marks his own. The contrast is deliberate. The mark of the beast is a counterfeit sign of belonging, just as beast-worship is a counterfeit religion and the beastly order is a counterfeit kingdom.

The Language of the Mark

Revelation 13:16-17 says, "And it causes all persons, the small and the great, and the rich and the poor, and the free and the slaves, that these should be given a mark on their right hand or on their forehead, and that no one should be able to buy or sell except the person having the mark, the name of the beast or the number of its name." This statement is clear in several important ways. First, the mark is universal in scope within the beast's domain. It reaches all classes of society. John lists small and great, rich and poor, free and slave. The point is that the beastly system seeks totalizing allegiance. It is not content with selective loyalty. It demands public conformity from the whole social order.

Second, the mark is placed on the right hand or forehead. These locations are not arbitrary. In Scripture, the forehead and hand often represent thought, identity, and action. Deuteronomy 6:6-8 commands Israel to keep Jehovah's words upon the heart and to bind them as a sign on the hand and as frontlets between the eyes. The imagery points to thought and conduct shaped by God's commandments. Revelation uses this biblical background in the opposite direction. The beast claims hand and forehead because he seeks to shape thought and conduct in the service of rebellion. The forehead points to identification, loyalty, and confessed belonging. The hand points to action, work, and practical participation. The mark therefore signifies the mind and life brought into conformity with the beastly order.

Third, the text joins the mark, the name of the beast, and the number of its name. This shows that the mark is not isolated from the beast's identity. It signifies belonging to the beast, bearing his claim, and standing under his authority. The mark is not merely a functional permit. It is a sign of association with the beast and with what he represents. This is why the text can speak of "the mark, the name of the beast, or the number of its name." These realities belong together. The mark signifies identification with the beastly order, and the number interprets the character of that order.

The Mark as Worshipful Allegiance

The most important fact about the mark of the beast is that it is inseparable from worship. Revelation 13 repeatedly says that the earth's inhabitants worship the dragon because he gave authority to the beast, and they worship the beast itself (Rev. 13:4, 8, 12, 15). The second beast performs signs to deceive those dwelling on the earth, tells them to make an image to the beast, and gives breath to the image so that it causes those who refuse to worship it to be killed (Rev. 13:13-15). Only after establishing this worship framework does the text mention the mark. The order matters. Worship comes first. The mark is the visible sign of submission to that worshipful order.

This guards against shallow interpretation. The mark of the beast is not first a matter of retail systems, personal documentation, or external mechanism. Those may become part of the coercive structure, as buying and selling clearly show, but they are not the theological center. The center is loyalty expressed through worship. Revelation 14 confirms this by saying, "If anyone worships the beast and its image, and receives a mark on his forehead or on his hand, he will also drink of the wine of the wrath of God" (Rev. 14:9-10). The receiving of the mark is bound directly to worship of the beast. This means the mark cannot be reduced to something involuntary or purely accidental in the moral sense the passage describes. It is bound up with beast-loyalty.

That does not mean the mark is only inward. Revelation clearly presents it as something that carries visible and social consequences. But the visible aspect rests upon a prior issue of allegiance. The anti-God order seeks to possess human beings in thought and action, to claim public conformity, and to attach participation in the world's system to idolatrous loyalty. This is why the mark belongs to worship first and economy second. The economic pressure is real, but it serves the deeper spiritual demand.

The Contrast with God's Seal

A proper understanding of the mark requires careful comparison with God's seal upon His servants. Revelation 7 shows four angels holding back destructive winds until the servants of God are sealed on their foreheads (Rev. 7:1-3). Revelation 14 presents the Lamb's people as having His name and His Father's name written on their foreheads. Revelation 22 says God's servants will see His face and His name will be on their foreheads (Rev. 22:4). This repeated imagery shows that God claims His people openly and permanently. They belong to Him, bear His name, and live under His authority.

The mark of the beast is the satanic imitation of that covenantal ownership. Just as God claims His people, the beast claims his worshipers. Just as God's name marks loyalty and belonging, the beast's mark signifies allegiance to the anti-God order. Just as the servants of God are preserved and identified, the beast's followers are likewise identified within the sphere of rebellion. The contrast is one of two masters, two worships, two identities, and two final outcomes. There is no neutrality in Revelation's moral universe. One either belongs to God and the Lamb or to the dragon and the beastly order.

This also explains why the mark carries such serious consequences. It is not a minor end-time curiosity. It reveals whom one serves. In Revelation 14, those who receive the mark are contrasted with those who keep the commandments of God and the faith of Jesus (Rev. 14:12). In Revelation 15, those victorious over the beast, its image, and the number of its name stand beside the glassy sea and sing the song of Moses and of the Lamb (Rev. 15:2-3). In Revelation 16, the bowl judgments fall in part upon those who have the mark of the beast and worship its image (Rev. 16:2). In Revelation 19, the beast and false prophet are destroyed, the false prophet being the one who deceived those who received the mark (Rev. 19:20). In Revelation 20, those who had not worshiped the beast or its image and had not received the mark reign with Christ (Rev. 20:4). The mark therefore functions throughout the Apocalypse as a sign of spiritual division and eschatological destiny.

The Economic Dimension of the Mark

Revelation says no one may buy or sell except the person having the mark, the name of the beast, or the number of its name (Rev. 13:17). This proves that the mark has practical and public consequences. It is not merely an inward attitude hidden from society. The beastly order uses commerce and participation in ordinary life as instruments of coercion. This fits the broader biblical pattern in which earthly powers seek to enforce conformity not only by violence, but by social and economic pressure. The mark therefore involves exclusion, penalty, and deprivation for those who refuse allegiance.

Yet even here, the economic dimension is not the starting point. It is the means by which the beastly order pressures the conscience. Those who refuse the beast are not merely financially inconvenienced. They are cut off because they will not submit to idolatrous authority. This makes the issue profoundly pastoral. The pressure of the mark is a pressure to compromise under threat of exclusion from ordinary life. The question becomes whether one will live by bread alone or by loyalty to God. Revelation's answer is that the faithful must be prepared to endure deprivation rather than surrender worship to the beast.

This also helps explain why the mark has often been misunderstood. Many readers begin with buying and selling and then work backward, treating the whole subject as though Scripture were mainly warning about a future mechanism of commerce. But the text itself begins with worship, proceeds to image and deception, and only then reaches buying and selling. The economic coercion is real, but it is subordinated to the theological issue of worshipful allegiance. To reverse that order is to misread the passage.

The Number of the Beast: 666

Revelation 13:18 says, "Here is the wisdom: Let the one having intelligence calculate the number of the beast, for it is a man's number, and its number is six hundred sixty-six." This verse has been a breeding ground for endless speculation. Yet the text itself gives several boundaries that the interpreter must respect. First, the number belongs to the beast. It interprets the beastly order and is attached to the mark, the name, and the identity of the beast. Second, John says, "Here is the wisdom," which means this requires discernment governed by revelation, not sensational imagination. Third, the number is "a man's number," or "the number of a man." This indicates that the number speaks of humanity in relation to the beastly system, not of divine perfection or sacred fullness.

The repeated six is significant. In biblical symbolism, seven often marks completeness, fullness, or divine perfection in the sense intended by the context. Six, falling short of seven, can signify incompleteness, creaturely inadequacy, and human limitation. The number 666 therefore most naturally points to intensified human rebellion, man raised to arrogant fullness in his own eyes while still falling short of God. The beast appears powerful, glorious, and worthy of allegiance, but his number exposes him. He is man in climactic defiance, not God. He is the mature anti-God order of man asserting itself in false greatness.

This does not mean the number has no connection to historical embodiment. Revelation's symbolism is not vague. Yet the theological meaning must govern all attempts at interpretation. The number is not given to encourage endless code-cracking across every generation. It is given to expose the character of the beastly order. Even when man exalts himself, organizes power, commands worship, and controls commerce, he remains creaturely, fallen, and destined for judgment. The beast is numbered precisely because he is not God. His false claims can be measured and exposed.

This reading also fits the larger thrust of Revelation. The beast is repeatedly shown as grand, terrifying, and world-dominating, yet always under divine limit. He is given authority, not self-originating authority. He blasphemes, but his doom is fixed. He gathers worshipers, but the Lamb conquers him. The number 666 therefore functions as part of that exposure. It reveals the beastly order as man in rebellion, not as an equal rival to God.

The Mark Is Not a Mere Accident

Because Revelation joins the mark so closely to worship, Scripture gives no support for treating the mark as a merely accidental condition imposed upon innocent people without moral significance. Revelation consistently presents the marked as those who follow the beastly order and those unmarked as those who remain loyal to God and the testimony of Jesus. The issue is not random exposure. It is allegiance under pressure.

This does not mean that every person who comes into contact with beastly systems has consciously articulated every theological implication of his actions. But the passage itself insists that the mark belongs to beast-worship and anti-God identification. It is not a morally empty label. The recipients are described as those who worship the beast and its image. The punishments that fall upon them are therefore judicial and moral, not arbitrary. This is another reason shallow technological interpretations fail. They often sever the mark from the conscience, from worship, and from covenant loyalty, treating it almost as though men stumble into it by procedural involvement alone. Revelation does not describe it that way.

The Mark and the Final Conflict

The mark of the beast belongs to the final conflict between the kingdom of God and the mature anti-God order. Revelation 13 does not describe an ordinary feature of history repeated in every age in the same form. The beastly pattern runs through history, but the mark in John's vision belongs to the final intensification of anti-God power. The dragon, the beast, the false prophet, the image, the mark, and the number all work together within the last battle for visible allegiance before the overthrow of the present beastly system.

This is why the mark must be placed within the sequence of Revelation. The beast rises, blasphemes, and persecutes. The false prophet deceives through signs. The image demands worship. The mark identifies allegiance. Judgment then falls upon the marked. The Lamb triumphs. The beast and false prophet are thrown into the lake of fire. Those who refused the mark reign with Christ. This sequence is part of the premillennial order of Revelation 19–20 and should be respected. The mark is not merely a symbol for generic worldliness across the whole church age. It belongs to the mature and climactic beastly order preceding the public triumph of Christ.

The Pastoral Meaning of the Mark

Revelation was given to churches, and the mark therefore has pastoral force. It teaches believers how to see the world and how to endure in it. The anti-God order does not demand loyalty only through arguments. It pressures through fear, exclusion, and control over ordinary life. It seeks visible conformity. It claims the right to define belonging and to punish dissent. The mark embodies this pressure. Therefore, the church must understand that the final test is not merely doctrinal in the abstract. It is practical, costly, and public.

This is why Revelation repeatedly blesses endurance. The saints conquer not by compromise, but by faithfulness. "Here is the endurance and the faith of the holy ones" appears precisely where beast-worship and the mark are being described (Rev. 13:10; 14:12). The church's task is to keep the commandments of God and the faith of Jesus even when the world order attaches survival and participation to false worship. The message is not that believers will escape all pressure before it comes. The message is that they must refuse the beastly claim upon hand and forehead, thought and action, conscience and conduct.

This pastoral emphasis also corrects a common error. Many discussions of the mark are dominated by fear rather than faithfulness. Men become preoccupied with identifying mechanisms while neglecting the central issue of worship. Revelation instead trains believers to ask: To whom does my loyalty belong? Whose name do I bear? Whose authority governs my thought and action? The mark of the beast matters because it represents a final answer to those questions in rebellion against God. The seal of God matters because it represents the true answer in covenant loyalty to Him.

The Mark, Babylon, and the Beastly Order

The mark also belongs to the wider anti-God system described elsewhere in Revelation. Babylon the Great intoxicates the nations with her immorality, luxury, and corruption. The kings of the earth commit fornication with her, and the merchants grow rich from her power (Rev. 18:3). This means the economic dimension of the mark is not isolated. It belongs to a world order in which commerce, pleasure, false religion, and political power are woven together in rebellion against God. The beast is not merely a state, and Babylon is not merely a city. Together they represent an organized anti-God civilization in its mature form. The mark is the sign of belonging to that civilization under the beast's direct claim.

This is why the people of God are told, "Get out of her, my people, if you do not want to share with her in her sins" (Rev. 18:4). The call is moral and spiritual separation from a doomed order. The faithful cannot belong to Babylon and to the holy city at the same time. They cannot bear the beast's mark and the Lamb's name. The mark therefore belongs to the larger issue of separation from the anti-God order and exclusive loyalty to God.

The Final Doom of Those Who Receive the Mark

Revelation speaks with severe clarity about the destiny of those who receive the mark. Revelation 14 says that those who worship the beast and receive his mark drink of the wine of God's wrath, poured out unmixed into the cup of His anger (Rev. 14:9-10). Revelation 16 records that a harmful and malignant sore comes upon the people who had the mark of the beast and who worshiped its image (Rev. 16:2). Revelation 19 says the false prophet deceived those who had received the mark, and both beast and false prophet are thrown alive into the lake of fire (Rev. 19:20). Revelation 20 contrasts the marked with those who refused the beast and therefore reign with Christ (Rev. 20:4).

These judgments must not be softened. Revelation is not embarrassed by divine wrath against idolatrous rebellion. The mark is not a harmless sign. It identifies those who have chosen the beast's order over the authority of God and the Lamb. The severity of the judgment reflects the seriousness of the rebellion. Yet even here, the purpose of the warning is pastoral. God reveals the end of the marked so that people may refuse the beast and remain faithful. The warning is not given to fascinate. It is given to summon endurance and loyalty.

Wisdom, Not Speculation

Revelation says, "Here is the wisdom" (Rev. 13:18). Wisdom is needed because the beastly order is deceptive. Outward power, signs, and economic control can make rebellion appear inevitable. But wisdom sees through the appearance. The beast is numbered. Babylon falls. The false prophet deceives only for a time. The mark signifies belonging to a doomed order. The Lamb stands on Mount Zion. The saints conquer. The wisdom of Revelation is therefore not cleverness in solving riddles for their own sake. It is spiritual discernment governed by the Word of God.

This means believers must resist two opposite errors. One is uncontrolled speculation, in which every new development is immediately identified as the mark without regard to context, worship, or the sequence of prophecy. The other is emptying the mark of all seriousness by making it only a vague symbol of generic badness. Wisdom avoids both. It keeps the mark tied to the final beastly order, to worshipful allegiance, to visible conformity, and to the economic coercion that serves false worship. It also keeps the mark under the larger truth that Christ will triumph and that the beastly order is temporary.

The Mark in the Light of the Lamb's Victory

The doctrine of the mark of the beast reaches its proper meaning only when read in the light of the Lamb's victory. Revelation does not end with the beast marking humanity. It ends with the Lamb reigning, the saints vindicated, evil judged, and the new creation established. The beast marks his followers, but God seals His servants. The beast excludes from buying and selling, but the Lamb grants access to the river of life. The beast's worshipers share in judgment, but the conquerors stand with the Lamb and reign with Him. The final issue is not how powerful the mark becomes, but how completely the beastly order is overthrown by Christ.

Therefore the mark of the beast must be understood as the visible sign of allegiance to the final anti-God order, attached to worship of the beast, enforced through deception and economic coercion, and exposing the character of the beastly system as man in climactic rebellion, numbered as 666. It is the counterfeit sign over against God's own seal. It claims thought and action, forehead and hand, name and loyalty. It belongs to the mature beastly order described in Revelation and meets its end when the Lamb conquers every rival.

The faithful response is not panic, nor careless speculation, but endurance, separation, and unwavering allegiance to God and to the testimony of Jesus. Revelation does not train the church to fear the mark more than it trusts Christ. It trains the church to see the beastly order for what it is: deceptive, coercive, rebellious, and doomed. The saints conquer because the Lamb conquers. Those who refuse the mark do not lose in the end. They reign with Christ, while the beastly order, however terrifying for a season, collapses beneath the judgment of the One whose name alone endures forever.

CHAPTER 6 Explaining the Great Tribulation

The Meaning of the Great Tribulation

The Great Tribulation is not a vague expression for all suffering in human history, nor is it merely a dramatic way of describing the general hardships believers face in a fallen world. Scripture does teach that the people of God experience tribulation in every age. Jesus says, "In the world you have tribulation" (John 16:33). Paul says, "Through many tribulations we must enter into the kingdom of God" (Acts 14:22). Yet the Great Tribulation spoken of in Matthew 24 is something more specific. It is a unique, climactic, unparalleled period of distress immediately connected to the final phase of the end of the age and the visible coming of the Son of Man.

Jesus states the matter plainly: "For then there will be great tribulation such as has not occurred since the beginning of the world until now, no, nor will occur again" (Matt. 24:21). Those words prevent the interpreter from flattening the term into the ordinary afflictions of all generations. This tribulation is distinguished by its intensity and uniqueness. It is not simply one more example of persecution among many. It belongs to the closing crisis of the present order of rebellion. It is part of the prophetic sequence that leads directly to the appearing of Christ in glory.

This is why the doctrine of the Great Tribulation must be treated with seriousness and precision. It belongs to the same framework as the signs of the end, the abomination of desolation, the rise of lawless rebellion, and the coming of the Son of Man. It does not stand alone. Daniel lays its groundwork, Jesus gives its clearest description, Paul places it within the apostasy and the man of lawlessness, and Revelation unveils its broader setting within the final conflict between the Lamb and the beastly order. When these passages are allowed to speak together, the Great Tribulation emerges as the concentrated time of end-time distress by which God brings the present evil order to its appointed crisis before the public triumph of Christ.

The Old Testament Foundation in Daniel

The clearest Old Testament background for the Great Tribulation is Daniel 12:1. There the prophet writes, "And during that time Michael will stand up, the great prince who is standing in behalf of the sons of your people. And there will certainly occur a time of distress such as has not been made to occur since there came to be a nation until that time. And during that time your people will escape, everyone who is found written down in the book." The language is unmistakable. Daniel speaks of a unique time of distress unlike anything before it. He also places that distress in direct connection with Michael's decisive action, the deliverance of God's people, and the resurrection hope that follows in Daniel 12:2.

This is not an accidental similarity to Jesus' words. It is the very prophetic foundation upon which Jesus builds. When Jesus speaks of the abomination of desolation spoken of through Daniel the prophet and then says there will be "great tribulation" unlike anything before or after, He is deliberately invoking Daniel's end-time pattern (Matt.

24:15, 21). That means the Great Tribulation must be read in continuity with Daniel's time of the end. It is not merely a general description of suffering. It belongs to the final prophetic crisis associated with the maturing of anti-God rebellion and the intervention of heaven on behalf of God's people.

Daniel's larger framework confirms this. Daniel 7 presents beastly powers persecuting the holy ones until the heavenly court sits in judgment and the kingdom is given to them (Dan. 7:21-22, 26-27). Daniel 8 describes a fierce ruler who throws truth to the ground and exalts himself before being broken "without hand" (Dan. 8:12, 25). Daniel 11 presents an arrogant king whose career moves toward an appointed end, and Daniel 12 follows with the unparalleled distress and deliverance. The Great Tribulation, then, belongs to the Danielic pattern of final beastly oppression, heavenly intervention, and kingdom transition. Any interpretation that ignores Daniel will inevitably weaken or distort the meaning of Jesus' words.

Jesus' Own Description of the Great Tribulation

The fullest New Testament description of the Great Tribulation comes from Jesus in the Olivet Discourse. After warning of false christs, wars, famines, earthquakes, persecution, apostasy, and worldwide witness, Jesus says, "Therefore when you catch sight of the disgusting thing that causes desolation, as spoken about through Daniel the prophet, standing in a holy place, let the reader use discernment, then let those in Judea begin fleeing to the mountains" (Matt. 24:15-16). He then gives urgent instructions showing that this moment marks a sudden and serious transition. There must be no delay, no return for possessions, and intense concern for those most vulnerable in that crisis (Matt. 24:17-20). Then comes the reason: "For then there will be great tribulation" (Matt. 24:21).

This sequence matters. The Great Tribulation is not the opening condition of the age. It is not simply everything bad that happens before Christ returns. It follows the abomination of desolation and marks the concentrated climax of the end-time conflict. Jesus presents it as the intensified phase that directly precedes the cosmic disturbances and the visible coming of the Son of Man (Matt. 24:29-31). Thus, the Great Tribulation is part of a defined prophetic order: deception and unrest characterize the broad last-days environment; the abomination appears; the Great Tribulation follows; then the heavenly signs and the public appearing of Christ arrive.

Jesus also says, "In fact, unless those days were cut short, no flesh would be saved; but on account of the chosen ones those days will be cut short" (Matt. 24:22). This statement reveals both the severity and the limit of the tribulation. It is so intense that unchecked continuation would mean total devastation. Yet it is also shortened by divine mercy for the sake of the chosen ones. This is a critical theological point. The Great Tribulation is not chaos outside God's control. It unfolds within His decree. He does not spare His people from the reality of the crisis altogether, but He does govern its length and outcome. The tribulation is therefore severe, but measured.

Jesus also links the Great Tribulation with intensified deception. In the same context He warns against false claims that Christ is here or there, whether in the wilderness or in inner rooms (Matt. 24:23-26). This means the tribulation is not only a time of suffering, but also of religious confusion, false hope, counterfeit salvation, and manipulative claims. The church must therefore not only endure hardship, but also remain anchored in truth. The final crisis attacks both body and conscience, both survival and worship.

The Great Tribulation and the Abomination of Desolation

Because Jesus places the Great Tribulation after the abomination of desolation, the relationship between the two must be carefully understood. The abomination signals a decisive profanation in relation to what is holy and marks the transition into the final concentrated crisis. It belongs to the anti-God order's mature defiance of God and its invasion of the sphere of worship. In Daniel, the language of abomination and desolation is tied to profanation, arrogant opposition, and final end-time conflict. In Jesus' discourse, it functions as a trigger event that calls for immediate flight and announces the beginning of unparalleled distress.

This means the Great Tribulation does not arise in a vacuum. It is connected to the maturing of lawless and beastly rebellion. The final crisis is not merely a natural disaster or a political war detached from spiritual meaning. It is the concentrated outworking of anti-God revolt against truth, worship, and the people of God. This is why the abomination and the tribulation belong together. The anti-God order reaches a point of intolerable profanation, and the resulting crisis brings history into its final convulsion before Christ's intervention.

This also helps explain why Scripture never treats the Great Tribulation as mere suffering for suffering's sake. It belongs to the exposure of evil. It reveals the beastly order for what it truly is. It strips away illusions of neutrality. It presses mankind toward visible allegiance either to God and the Lamb or to the rebellious anti-God system. In this sense, the tribulation is both judicial and revelatory. It brings the moral nature of the final conflict into plain view.

Distinguishing General Tribulation From the Great Tribulation

A major interpretive error occurs when every biblical reference to tribulation is treated as though it referred to the same thing in the same way. Scripture uses tribulation language broadly and specifically. Broadly, tribulation refers to the affliction, pressure, suffering, and opposition experienced by God's people in a fallen world. This is a normal feature of Christian life in the present age. Jesus promises tribulation in the world. Paul says believers enter the kingdom through many tribulations. Revelation addresses congregations already facing tribulation, poverty, imprisonment, and persecution (Rev. 2:9-10).

But the Great Tribulation of Matthew 24 is not simply that broad reality. It is specific, climactic, and unparalleled. Jesus' wording forbids reducing it to the ongoing hardships of the entire church age. The phrase "such as has not occurred since the world's beginning until now, no, nor will occur again" requires a unique crisis. Daniel 12:1 says the same in Old Testament form. This means that while believers always live under pressure of some kind, the Great Tribulation is the intensified final distress associated with the time of the end.

This distinction matters because if all tribulation is treated as the Great Tribulation, then Jesus' signs lose their force, the Danielic background is flattened, and the prophetic sequence becomes indistinct. On the other hand, if the Great Tribulation is pushed so far into the future that it has no relation to the biblical patterns of apostasy, lawlessness, and beastly oppression, the church is left unprepared for how the final crisis develops. The right reading preserves both truths: the church always knows tribulation in the broad sense, but the Great Tribulation is the final, unparalleled, concentrated form of end-time distress.

The Great Tribulation and the Man of Lawlessness

Paul does not use the exact phrase "Great Tribulation" in 2 Thessalonians 2, yet his teaching belongs to the same prophetic horizon. He speaks of the apostasy, the man of lawlessness, the mystery of lawlessness already at work, deceptive signs, and the final destruction of the lawless one by the manifestation of Christ's presence (2 Thess. 2:3-10). This places the church in a period of intensified deception and rebellion before the visible intervention of Christ. Paul's sequence therefore harmonizes with Jesus' discourse.

The apostasy Paul describes belongs to the broad context of the Great Tribulation because the final crisis is not merely physical distress. It is spiritual revolt, doctrinal corruption, and the maturing of anti-God rebellion. The man of lawlessness exalts himself in the sphere of worship, publicly showing himself to be a god (2 Thess. 2:4). Such self-exaltation belongs naturally within the same final crisis as the abomination of desolation and the beastly demand for worship in Revelation 13. The Great Tribulation is therefore not only about persecution from outside, but also about the climactic eruption of apostate lawlessness and false worship from within the professing sphere.

This means the tribulation must be understood as a crisis involving both suffering and deception. The faithful are pressured from without and assaulted by lies from within. Paul's emphasis on lying signs and unrighteous deception shows that the final crisis includes counterfeit religious power. Therefore the people of God must endure not only by courage, but also by love of the truth. The Great Tribulation is a time when only those rooted in apostolic truth and loyal to Christ can remain unmoved.

The Great Tribulation and the Beastly Order

Revelation gives the broader apocalyptic setting of the final crisis. While the exact phrase "Great Tribulation" appears in Revelation 7:14 in relation to those coming out of "the great tribulation," the book as a whole shows the environment in which that tribulation unfolds. The dragon rages against the woman and the rest of her offspring who keep God's commandments and hold to the testimony of Jesus (Rev. 12:17). The beast from the sea blasphemes God and wages war against the holy ones (Rev. 13:6-7). The beast from the earth deceives the earth's inhabitants, enforces worship of the first beast, and compels the mark of allegiance (Rev. 13:11-17). Babylon intoxicates the nations while persecuting the holy ones and prophets (Rev. 17:6; 18:24). Together these passages reveal the anti-God order at its most mature and aggressive form.

This is the world of the Great Tribulation. It is a world in which the dragon works through beastly political and religious powers, truth is assaulted, worship is corrupted, and the faithful face exclusion, persecution, and death. The tribulation is therefore not merely a period of calamity in the abstract. It is the concentrated pressure of the final anti-God order upon the people of God and upon the world as God brings history to judgment.

Revelation 7 is especially important because it speaks of a great crowd "coming out of the great tribulation" and identifies them as those who have washed their robes and made them white in the blood of the Lamb (Rev. 7:14). This shows that the Great Tribulation is not merely a doctrine of wrath upon the world. It is also a doctrine of preservation, cleansing, and vindication for those who belong to the

Lamb. The people of God are not forgotten within the crisis. They come through it by divine mercy and redemptive cleansing.

Is the Great Tribulation God's Wrath or Man's Rage?

The Great Tribulation cannot be reduced entirely to one side of the question. On the one hand, the final crisis includes the rage of Satan, the hostility of the beastly order, and the persecution of the faithful. Revelation makes this plain. The dragon is enraged, the beast wages war, the false prophet deceives, and Babylon sheds the blood of God's people. On the other hand, the final crisis also unfolds under the sovereign judgments of God. The seals, trumpets, and bowls are not independent disasters. They proceed from heaven. The tribulation therefore takes place within divine government and within the movement of God's judgments against a rebellious world.

This means the Great Tribulation includes both the rage of evil and the wrath of God in measured judicial action. It is the final crisis in which evil reaches maturity and God responds in righteousness, while preserving and vindicating His people. The church must not think in simplistic alternatives, as though the tribulation were only Satan's activity or only God's judgment. Scripture presents the final crisis as a convergence: beastly oppression intensifies, deception matures, and divine judgments advance toward the overthrow of the present order.

That also explains why the tribulation is so severe. It is not merely one historical conflict among many. It is the final concentration of rebellion under the hand of divine judgment. The powers of darkness press their claims with unusual intensity, yet they do so under limits set by Jehovah, and only until the appointed manifestation of Christ.

The Great Tribulation Is Cut Short

One of the most comforting truths in Jesus' teaching is that the days of the Great Tribulation are shortened for the sake of the chosen ones (Matt. 24:22). This statement reveals the mercy of God within judgment. The tribulation is not allowed to continue indefinitely. The same Lord who foretells the crisis also fixes its boundary. The chosen ones are not beyond His care. Even in the most severe distress, He remains the Shepherd of His people.

This is consistent with the rest of prophetic Scripture. Daniel's times are measured. The little horn is allowed to wear down the holy ones only for "a time, times, and half a time" (Dan. 7:25). The trampling and profanation in Daniel 8 are likewise bounded by divine answer. Revelation repeatedly assigns periods and limits to beastly activity. The beast is given authority for forty-two months (Rev. 13:5). The nations tread the holy city for forty-two months (Rev. 11:2). The woman is nourished in the wilderness for a measured period (Rev. 12:6, 14). The point in all these texts is the same: evil is active, but timed. The tribulation is terrible, but governed. God never relinquishes control.

This truth has immense pastoral significance. The Great Tribulation is not meant to drive believers into despair. It is meant to call them to endurance under the assurance that their God has numbered the days, measured the rage of evil, and guaranteed the final outcome. The shortening of the days does not mean the crisis is unreal. It means mercy operates even within judgment.

The Great Tribulation and the Gathering of the Chosen Ones

Jesus places the Great Tribulation immediately before the cosmic disturbances and the visible coming of the Son of Man. "Immediately after the tribulation of those days," He says, "the sun will be darkened, and the moon will not give its light, and the stars will fall from heaven" (Matt. 24:29). Then He speaks of the Son of Man coming with power and great glory and of the gathering of His chosen ones by the angels (Matt. 24:30-31). This sequence is direct and powerful. The tribulation is followed by divine world-shaking signs, and then by the public appearing of Christ and the gathering of His people.

This has major implications. It means the Great Tribulation is not separated from Christ's visible return by an entirely different eschatological program. It belongs immediately before that appearing. It also means the gathering of the chosen ones is connected with Christ's open manifestation, not with a hidden secret event before the tribulation. Paul's teaching in 1 Thessalonians 4:16-17 and 2 Thessalonians 2:1-8 harmonizes with this pattern. The Lord descends, the dead in Christ rise, the living faithful are gathered, and the lawless one is destroyed by the appearance of Christ's presence. Scripture presents a unified sequence, not a fragmented one.

Thus the Great Tribulation functions as the final crisis through which the faithful pass into vindication and resurrection hope. It is not the last word. It is the final convulsion of the present age before the King appears.

The Great Crowd Coming Out of the Great Tribulation

Revelation 7:14 gives one of the most encouraging pictures related to the Great Tribulation. John sees a great crowd from all nations, tribes, peoples, and tongues standing before the throne and before the Lamb, clothed in white robes and holding palm branches. When asked who they are, he is told, "These are the ones who come out of the great tribulation, and they have washed their robes and made them white in the blood of the Lamb." This text shows that the Great Tribulation, though severe, is not the destruction of the faithful. They come out of it. Their white robes signify cleansing, acceptance, and vindication through the sacrifice of Christ.

This is deeply important. The Great Tribulation is often spoken of only in tones of dread. Revelation refuses to leave the matter there. Those who belong to the Lamb are not abandoned in the crisis. Their deliverance is not based on their own strength, but on the blood of the Lamb. They emerge not because they outmaneuvered the beastly order, but because they were redeemed, kept, and vindicated by God. This places the whole doctrine firmly within the gospel. The final crisis is real, but the saving power of Christ is greater.

The following verses intensify that hope. They stand before God, render Him sacred service, hunger and thirst no more, and are shepherded by the Lamb, while God wipes every tear from their eyes (Rev. 7:15-17). The Great Tribulation, then, leads not to ultimate defeat but to worship, relief, and divine comfort for the faithful. This is why prophecy is given—to strengthen endurance through hope.

The Great Tribulation and the Need for Endurance

Because the Great Tribulation includes persecution, deception, pressure, and public conflict, Scripture repeatedly connects it with endurance. Jesus says, "The one who has endured to the end is the one who will be saved" (Matt. 24:13). Revelation says, "Here is where it means endurance for the holy ones" (Rev. 13:10). Again, after warning against worship of the beast and receiving its mark, Revelation adds, "Here is where it means endurance for the holy ones, those who observe the commandments of God and the faith of Jesus" (Rev. 14:12). The consistent message is clear. The final crisis does not call for speculation, but for steadfast obedience.

Endurance here is not passive resignation. It is active covenant loyalty. It means refusing the beastly order, rejecting false worship, keeping the commandments of God, and holding fast to the testimony of Jesus under pressure. The Great Tribulation is therefore not merely an event to be identified. It is a crisis through which faithfulness must be proved. The church must be trained to see that the final issue is allegiance, not comfort.

This is why the doctrine of the Great Tribulation is pastorally necessary. It teaches believers not to be surprised by the hostility of the world, not to be misled by false claims of peace, not to imagine that the kingdom comes through compromise with the beastly order, and not to surrender hope when evil seems most intense. The tribulation shows what the world truly is apart from Christ. Endurance shows who truly belongs to Christ within that world.

The Great Tribulation and the Nearness of Deliverance

Luke's version of the Olivet Discourse includes an important word of encouragement: "As these things start to occur, straighten up and lift up your heads, because your deliverance is getting near" (Luke 21:28). This does not minimize the severity of the final crisis. It reinterprets it for the faithful. What terrifies the rebellious world signals approaching deliverance for those who belong to Christ. The Great Tribulation therefore has opposite meanings depending on one's relation to God. For the rebellious, it is the beginning of final exposure. For the faithful, it is the final crisis before rescue, vindication, and kingdom transition.

This is why Jesus can command watchfulness rather than terror. The tribulation is severe, but not ultimate. The world order is shaken, but only because it is about to be judged. The saints suffer, but only until the Son of Man appears. The signs do not point to chaos reigning forever. They point to Christ being near, at the doors. Thus the church must read the Great Tribulation not only as warning, but as hope-filled warning. It is the last storm before the King appears.

The Great Tribulation in Harmony With the Whole Prophetic Witness

When all the relevant passages are held together, the biblical doctrine becomes clear. Daniel establishes a unique end-time distress connected with Michael's intervention and deliverance. Jesus identifies this as the Great Tribulation following the abomination of desolation and preceding His visible coming. Paul places the church in the same final environment of apostasy, lawless self-exaltation, deception, and the eventual destruction of the lawless one by Christ's appearing. Revelation unveils the dragon, the beast, the false prophet, Babylon, the mark, and the great crowd coming out of the Great Tribulation, all within the final conflict that leads to the triumph of the Lamb.

This harmony matters because the doctrine must not be built on one isolated text alone. Scripture presents one coherent picture. The Great Tribulation is not the entire church age, yet it does arise from patterns already at work in the age. It is not merely social collapse, but the concentrated final conflict of anti-God power and divine judgment. It is not disconnected from Christ's return, but immediately precedes His visible appearing and the gathering of His chosen ones. It is not outside God's control, but measured, shortened, and governed by His decree. And it is not the defeat of the faithful, but the last severe crisis through which they pass into vindication, cleansing, and deliverance.

Living in View of the Great Tribulation

The doctrine of the Great Tribulation calls for several practical responses. It calls for discernment, because deception will intensify. It calls for courage, because persecution and exclusion will accompany the final crisis. It calls for holiness, because lawlessness and apostasy will spread. It calls for steadfast love of the truth, because the lie will come with power and impressive signs. It calls for watchfulness, because the world will continue in complacency until judgment overtakes it. And it calls for hope, because the Great Tribulation is not the end of God's people, but the last convulsion of the present age before Christ appears.

Those who understand the doctrine rightly will not romanticize suffering, but neither will they be surprised by the severity of the final conflict. They will not confuse the broad tribulations of Christian life with the unique final crisis, yet they will understand that present faithfulness prepares the church for future endurance. They will not be driven into fearful obsession, because they know the days are shortened for the sake of the chosen ones. And they will not treat the tribulation as an independent horror detached from redemption, because they know the great crowd comes out of it with robes made white in the blood of the Lamb.

The Great Tribulation, then, is the concentrated, unparalleled, end-time distress brought about by the maturing of anti-God rebellion and unfolding under the judicial sovereignty of Jehovah, immediately preceding the visible coming of Christ and the gathering of His chosen ones. It is severe, but measured. It is terrifying, but not ultimate. It is the final crisis of the present rebellious order, and beyond it stands the Son of Man, coming with power and great glory. That is why the faithful endure. The tribulation is great, but the Lamb is greater, and His victory is certain.

CHAPTER 7 Explaining Armageddon

The Meaning of Armageddon

Few biblical terms have been more widely used and more poorly understood than Armageddon. In popular speech it often means any catastrophic war, global disaster, nuclear exchange, or final collapse of civilization. Scripture uses the word far more carefully. The term appears directly in Revelation 16:16: "And they gathered them together to the place that is called in Hebrew Har–Magedon." That single occurrence has generated enormous speculation, yet the inspired context itself provides the controlling meaning. Armageddon is not merely a human war among nations for political dominance. It is the divinely appointed gathering of the kings of the whole inhabited earth for the war of the great day of God the Almighty (Rev. 16:14). It is therefore a theological, judicial, and eschatological event. The final issue is not who rules among men, but whether rebellious mankind can stand when Jehovah acts openly through His Christ.

This means Armageddon must be understood within the broader framework of Revelation 16–19 and in harmony with Daniel, the Olivet Discourse, 2 Thessalonians 2, and the Old Testament Day of Jehovah prophecies. It is the climax of the present anti-God order, the concentration of beastly rebellion, and the point at which the gathered powers of the world meet the direct intervention of God in Christ. Armageddon is not the whole end-time program. It is the climactic conflict that brings the present rebellious order to its decisive overthrow before the thousand-year reign described in Revelation 20. The sequence matters. The beast and false prophet are judged, Satan is bound, the holy ones reign with Christ, and only after that millennium does the final post-millennial rebellion occur. Armageddon, therefore, is not the end of all divine action. It is the judicial battle that closes the present age of beastly rebellion and opens the millennial administration of Christ.

The name itself must also be handled with care. The Hebrew form Har–Magedon is usually understood as "Mountain of Megiddo," though Megiddo in the Old Testament is more directly associated with a plain or valley region than with a mountain. That tension signals that John is not merely giving a literal military map point for future armies to occupy in a conventional geopolitical way. Revelation is a book of signs, and place names often carry theological and historical associations beyond geography alone. Megiddo evokes a region of decisive battles in Israel's history, including major conflicts and judgments under the old covenant order. The name therefore functions symbolically and theologically. It points to the place of decisive divine confrontation and judgment, the battlefield of history brought to its appointed climax under God's decree. The stress falls not on cartographic precision, but on the certainty of the gathering and the certainty of the outcome.

The Context of Armageddon in Revelation

Armageddon is introduced in Revelation 16 during the pouring out of the seven bowls of the wrath of God. These bowls are not random disasters. They are judicial acts proceeding from heaven against a rebellious world. The sixth bowl is especially significant: "And the sixth one poured out his bowl on the great river Euphrates, and its water was dried up, so that the way might be prepared for the kings from the rising of the sun" (Rev. 16:12). Then John sees "three unclean inspired expressions that looked like frogs" come out of the mouth of the dragon, the beast, and the false prophet. These are "inspired expressions of demons" that perform signs and go out to the kings of the whole inhabited earth "to gather them together to the war of the great day of God the Almighty" (Rev. 16:13-14). Verse 16 then states that they gathered them to the place called Armageddon.

This context is decisive. Armageddon is not introduced as a merely human political coalition formed by ordinary diplomacy. It is demonic gathering under divine permission for a divinely appointed war. The powers of rebellion are drawn together by deceptive spirits because God has ordained that they meet their end in one final confrontation. This immediately places Armageddon in continuity with Old Testament passages where Jehovah gathers nations for judgment. Joel says, "I will gather all the nations and bring them down to the valley of Jehoshaphat; and I will enter into judgment with them there" (Joel 3:2). Zechariah says, "I will gather all the nations against Jerusalem to the war" (Zech. 14:2). The nations gather in arrogance and hostility, but their gathering serves the judicial purpose of God. Revelation takes up that same pattern in climactic form.

The mention of the Euphrates being dried up also invites scriptural comparison. In the Old Testament, the drying up of waters could prepare the way for conquest and judgment. The Euphrates itself carried symbolic importance as a great boundary river associated with imperial power, especially in relation to Babylon. In Revelation the drying up of the Euphrates prepares the way for the kings from the rising of the sun. Whether one sees in this a direct symbolic reversal of protective boundaries or a broader image of providential preparation, the main point is that obstacles to the final gathering are removed. God is preparing the stage for the final confrontation. The demonic spirits gather the kings, but they do so within a sequence already governed by the wrath of God.

It is equally important that the dragon, beast, and false prophet stand behind the gathering. Armageddon belongs to the final anti-God coalition. The dragon is Satanic power. The beast is the mature political order of rebellion. The false prophet is the deceptive religious power that directs men into beast-worship. Their unclean inspired expressions resemble frogs, which evokes uncleanness, plague imagery, and repulsive spiritual pollution. The final war is therefore not a neutral clash of civilizations. It is satanically energized hostility against God and against His Christ, expressed through a gathered coalition of rebellious earthly rulers.

Armageddon and the Day of Jehovah

Armageddon is called "the war of the great day of God the Almighty" (Rev. 16:14). That phrase immediately links it to the biblical doctrine of the Day of Jehovah, or the Day of the Lord. Throughout the prophets, the Day of Jehovah is the time when God intervenes in history in judgment, exposing pride, punishing wickedness, delivering His people, and establishing His own righteous rule. Isaiah speaks of the day of Jehovah as cruel, with fury and burning anger, to make the land an object of horror and to annihilate sinners from it (Isa. 13:9). Joel describes it as great and very fear-inspiring, asking, "Who can endure it?" (Joel 2:11). Zephaniah calls it a day of wrath, distress, devastation, darkness, trumpet blast, and battle cry against fortified cities (Zeph. 1:14-16). These passages do not merely refer to local judgments in a flat way; they also build a cumulative theology of divine intervention that reaches its climax in the final day of judgment.

The New Testament continues this doctrine. Paul says, "The day of Jehovah is coming exactly as a thief in the night" (1 Thess. 5:2). Peter says, "Jehovah's day will come as a thief, in which the heavens will pass away with a roar" (2 Pet. 3:10). Jesus' own teaching in Matthew 24 places the visible coming of the Son of Man after the Great Tribulation and after cosmic disturbances that echo Old Testament Day of Jehovah language (Matt. 24:29-31). Therefore, Armageddon belongs to this larger biblical reality. It is the climactic military-juridical expression of the Day of Jehovah in relation to the gathered kings of the earth and the beastly order they represent.

This means Armageddon cannot be reduced to one more war in ordinary history. It is the Day of God reaching its judicial climax against the anti-God coalition. It is not man successfully initiating a final revolt on equal terms with heaven. It is rebellious mankind being gathered, exposed, and crushed under the intervention of Christ. Psalm 2 already laid the theological foundation: the nations rage and the peoples mutter empty things; the kings of the earth take their stand against Jehovah and against His Anointed, yet Jehovah laughs and installs His King on Zion (Ps. 2:1-6). The Son is given the nations as His inheritance and breaks them with an iron scepter (Ps. 2:8-9). Armageddon is the Revelation form of this Psalm 2 reality. The kings gather against God's Christ, and the result is not divine uncertainty, but divine overthrow.

Armageddon Is Not a Mere Human World War

One of the most common misunderstandings about Armageddon is that it refers simply to a human war among nations in which God is only indirectly involved, or to a final military contest between earthly blocs of power. Scripture does not present it that way. The kings are gathered by demonic influence, but they are gathered for "the war of the great day of God the Almighty." The primary combatant is God in Christ. Revelation 19 makes this explicit. Heaven opens, and John sees a white horse whose rider is called Faithful and True, and "he judges and carries on war in righteousness" (Rev. 19:11). His eyes are a fiery flame, many diadems are on His head, and from His mouth projects a sharp long sword "so that he may strike the nations with it, and he will shepherd them with an iron rod" (Rev. 19:15). He is called "The Word of God" and also "King of kings and Lord of lords" (Rev. 19:13, 16). The scene is not one of balanced military uncertainty. It is one of heavenly intervention and royal judgment.

The enemies in Revelation 19 are the beast, the kings of the earth, and their armies, gathered to wage war with the rider on the horse and with his army (Rev. 19:19). This is the clearest narrative expansion of the Armageddon gathering. The kings are gathered, they stand in opposition to Christ, and they are decisively defeated. The beast and false prophet are seized and thrown alive into the lake of fire, while the rest are killed by the long sword that comes from the mouth of the rider (Rev. 19:20-21). Armageddon is therefore not merely man fighting man. It is man in rebellion attempting to stand against the revealed Christ and being destroyed by Him.

This also means Armageddon should not be confused with every regional war in the Middle East, nor should it be identified simplistically with modern military anxieties detached from the text. Revelation gives its own interpretive controls. Armageddon involves the dragon, the beast, the false prophet, the gathered kings of the earth, the Day of God, and the visible warfare of Christ in righteousness. It belongs to the mature anti-God order and to the visible intervention of the Son of God. Therefore, while ordinary wars may prepare the moral and political environment of the last days, Armageddon itself is the final God-centered confrontation, not merely the continuation of normal geopolitical conflict.

The Gathering of the Kings of the Earth

Revelation emphasizes the gathering of "the kings of the whole inhabited earth" (Rev. 16:14). This universal language matters. Armageddon is not a local tribal conflict confined to one nation. It is the gathered political order of the rebellious world. Revelation often uses kings of the earth as representatives of organized human power in opposition to God. In Revelation 17 they commit fornication with Babylon and hand over authority to the beast (Rev. 17:2, 12-13). In Revelation 18 they mourn Babylon's fall because they shared in her corrupt order (Rev. 18:9-10). In Revelation 19 they are gathered with their armies against Christ. The kings of the earth therefore represent the political dimension of the anti-God system in its mature and united form.

This should not be read as though every earthly government in all history is equally and identically Armageddon-ready at all times. The book shows development, concentration, and final alignment. The beastly order matures. Babylon reaches full corruption. The false prophet deceives. Demonic spirits gather. The kings yield themselves to the final anti-God coalition. Armageddon is the culmination of that process. It is the end of beastly world-rule in its final unified opposition to God.

This gathering also fulfills a wider prophetic pattern. Joel 3 speaks of the nations being aroused and coming up to the valley of Jehoshaphat, where Jehovah sits to judge them all around (Joel 3:12). Zechariah 12–14 repeatedly presents the nations gathered against Jerusalem and then defeated by Jehovah's intervention. Ezekiel 38–39 describes Gog and his hordes being drawn against the land only to be destroyed by divine judgment. These passages differ in imagery and detail, but they share a pattern of international rebellion gathered by divine providence for final judgment. Revelation 16 and 19 stand as the climactic New Testament unveiling of that pattern.

The Meaning of Har–Magedon

The name Har–Magedon has prompted endless debate, but the immediate task is not to solve every linguistic detail beyond what Scripture itself supports. The basic force is that John uses a Hebrew-based name with deep battle associations. Megiddo was the site or region of significant Old Testament conflicts, including the defeat of Sisera's forces in the days of Deborah and Barak (Judg. 4–5), the death of King Ahaziah in relation to Jehu's judgment (2 Ki. 9:27), and the death of Josiah at Megiddo (2 Ki. 23:29-30; 2 Chron. 35:22). Thus Megiddo evokes decisive battle, kings, judgment, and national turning points.

Yet Revelation's use of "mountain" with Megiddo suggests that the place name carries symbolic-theological force rather than functioning merely as a military coordinate. The Old Testament does not prominently speak of a Mount Megiddo in the ordinary geographical sense. John's form therefore encourages readers to think in terms of prophetic significance, not mere battlefield mapping. Armageddon is the place-name of the final decisive divine confrontation. It evokes the memory of historic judgments and gathers them into the eschatological climax. Just as Babylon in Revelation is more than one city and stands for the mature world-order in rebellion, so Armageddon is more than a battlefield reference and stands for the final appointed site of divine overthrow.

That symbolic force does not make it unreal. On the contrary, it heightens its reality. Armageddon signifies the final battlefield of God's judgment upon the kings of the earth. It is a real eschatological confrontation expressed through a theologically loaded place name. Scripture often does this. Zion is both a place and a theological center. Babylon is both historical and symbolic. Egypt can function both historically and typologically as bondage and oppression. Armageddon belongs in this pattern. It is the name by which Revelation designates the final war of the great day of God.

Armageddon and the Return of Christ

Armageddon cannot be separated from the visible return of Christ. Revelation 16 gathers the kings. Revelation 19 reveals the rider on the white horse destroying them. The two passages belong together. Likewise, Matthew 24 says that after the Great Tribulation the sign of the Son of Man appears, all the tribes of the earth mourn, and they see the Son of Man coming on the clouds of heaven with power and great glory (Matt. 24:29-30). 2 Thessalonians 2 says the lawless one is destroyed by the manifestation of Christ's presence (2 Thess. 2:8). These passages converge. The final anti-God order meets its end at Christ's appearing, not before, not after in some unrelated sequence, but at the public manifestation of His authority.

This has major doctrinal importance. Armageddon is not a battle after the millennium. Revelation 20 clearly places the thousand-year reign after the destruction of the beast and false prophet in Revelation 19. Satan is then bound so that he may not deceive the nations until the thousand years are ended (Rev. 20:1-3). Therefore Armageddon belongs before the millennium. It is the climactic battle that clears the way for the thousand-year kingdom administration of Christ and those who reign with Him.

This also means Armageddon is not a secret event invisible to the world. Revelation 19 is public, royal, and judicial. Christ appears with heaven opened, many diadems, and the armies of heaven following Him. The birds are summoned to the great evening meal of God to consume the flesh of kings and mighty men (Rev. 19:17-18). The imagery is severe, but the meaning is unmistakable: the kings of the earth are publicly overthrown. Armageddon is therefore part of the visible Second Coming, not an invisible phase hidden from the world.

Armageddon and the Destruction of the Beastly Order

The immediate result of Armageddon in Revelation is the destruction of the beast and false prophet and the slaughter of the gathered armies. This means Armageddon ends the present anti-God political-religious order in its mature form. The beast, who blasphemes God and wages war against the holy ones, is seized. The false prophet, who performed signs and deceived those who received the mark, is seized with him. Both are thrown alive into the lake of fire that burns with sulfur (Rev. 19:20). This is decisive and irreversible judgment against the head structures of end-time rebellion.

The rest are killed by the sword proceeding from the mouth of Christ (Rev. 19:21). Again, the symbolism must be read according to its theological force. Christ's mouth signifies His sovereign judicial word. He does not need conventional weapons. His authority destroys. The same Word by whom God created now judges. The image fulfills Isaiah 11:4 and confirms that the Messiah's victory is effortless in comparison with the pretensions of the gathered kings. Armageddon is not a close contest. It is the crushing of rebellion by the King whose right to rule has already been established by God.

This overthrow also answers the long conflict of Revelation. The dragon empowers the beast. The false prophet directs worship. Babylon intoxicates and corrupts. The kings join the rebellion. The holy ones suffer. At Armageddon, all of it comes under judgment. The beastly order falls. Therefore Armageddon is not merely a military episode. It is the theological collapse of the final anti-God world system.

Armageddon and the Vindication of the Holy Ones

Armageddon is also the vindication of the holy ones. Daniel 7 says the little horn made war with the holy ones and prevailed over them "until the Ancient of Days came and judgment itself was given in favor of the holy ones of the Supreme One" (Dan. 7:21-22). Revelation echoes this pattern. The beast wages war on the holy ones (Rev. 13:7), Babylon is drunk with the blood of the holy ones (Rev. 17:6), and the souls under the altar cry out for vindication (Rev. 6:9-11). Armageddon is the answer to those cries. It is the point at which God openly judges the persecuting order and vindicates those who remained faithful to the Lamb.

This vindication is not merely emotional comfort. It is historical and judicial. The powers that oppressed the people of God are overthrown. The slander against the faithful is answered by the appearing of Christ. The beast's temporary success is ended. Revelation 19 begins with heaven rejoicing that God has judged the great harlot who corrupted the earth and has avenged on her the blood of His slaves (Rev. 19:1-2). Thus Armageddon is not an isolated war scene tacked onto the end of Revelation. It is part of God's righteous answer to the suffering and faithfulness of His people.

This also explains why the saints in Revelation are called to endurance. They are not promised exemption from all conflict before the end. They are promised vindication at the end. Armageddon means the world does not have the last word about the people of God. Christ does. The kingdoms of the earth, however powerful for a time, do not define the future. The Lamb conquers them, and those with Him are called and chosen and faithful (Rev. 17:14).

Armageddon Is Not the Final Rebellion of Revelation 20

A crucial distinction must be maintained between Armageddon and the final rebellion after the thousand years in Revelation 20:7-10. These are not the same event. Armageddon occurs in the context of the beast, false prophet, and gathered kings before Satan is bound. Revelation 20 then shows Satan bound for a thousand years so that he may not mislead the nations until the thousand years are ended. After the thousand years, he is released, goes out to mislead the nations in the four corners of the earth, Gog and Magog, to gather them for the war, and they surround the camp of the holy ones and the beloved city. Fire comes down out of heaven and devours them, and Satan is thrown into the lake of fire where the beast and false prophet already are (Rev. 20:7-10).

The differences are obvious and important. In Armageddon, the beast and false prophet are active and are then cast into the lake of fire. In the post-millennial rebellion, the beast and false prophet are already in the lake of fire and Satan joins them only after the thousand years. Armageddon occurs before Satan's binding; the Gog and Magog rebellion occurs after Satan's release. Armageddon opens the way for the millennium; the final rebellion comes at its close and is followed by the great white throne. Therefore these cannot be the same battle retold in two forms. The chronological order of Revelation 19–20 must be respected.

This distinction matters because it preserves the premillennial structure of Revelation. Christ returns in judgment, destroys the beastly order at Armageddon, binds Satan, reigns for a thousand years with His holy ones, then permits a final rebellion which is also crushed, and only then comes the great white throne and the final phase of judgment. Armageddon therefore belongs to the transition from the present age into the millennial reign, not to the close of that reign.

Armageddon and the Prophetic Pattern of Jehovah's War

Armageddon should also be understood in light of the biblical pattern of Jehovah's war. In the Old Testament, God often fights for His people and against arrogant powers that oppose Him. At the Red Sea, Jehovah says, "Jehovah will fight for you, and you yourselves will keep silent" (Ex. 14:14). The song of Moses declares, "Jehovah is a mighty warrior" (Ex. 15:3). In Joshua, Judges, Samuel, Kings, and the prophets, divine warfare repeatedly appears as the overthrow of proud enemies by God's action rather than by human strength alone. Yet all these earlier wars were partial and anticipatory. They looked forward to the final day when Jehovah would intervene openly against the gathered rebellious nations.

Armageddon is the climactic fulfillment of this theme. The rider on the white horse "judges and carries on war in righteousness" (Rev. 19:11). This is not war for ambition, revenge, or conquest in the sinful human sense. It is war in righteousness. Christ wages war because God's holiness, truth, and kingdom rights require judgment against the final anti-God order. Therefore Armageddon must never be sentimentalized away. It is severe because the rebellion it judges is severe. It is decisive because God does not preserve evil as an eternal counter-kingdom alongside righteousness. The beastly order must be overthrown for the kingdom of God to proceed into its next revealed phase.

Armageddon and the Call to Watchfulness

Revelation inserts a striking word from Christ right in the middle of the sixth bowl narrative: "Look! I am coming as a thief. Happy is the one who stays awake and keeps his outer garments, so that he may not walk naked and people look at his shame" (Rev. 16:15). This beatitude is placed between the demonic gathering of the kings and the statement that they are gathered to Armageddon. The placement is highly significant. Armageddon is not only a doctrine of judgment upon the nations; it is also a call to watchfulness for God's people.

The image of staying awake and keeping one's garments recalls Jesus' repeated warnings in the Gospels about watchfulness. It also reflects the priestly and moral imagery of avoiding shame and remaining prepared before God. In other words, the doctrine of Armageddon is not given merely so that believers will know how the world ends. It is given so they will remain spiritually alert, morally clean, and loyally prepared for Christ's appearing. This again shows the pastoral function of prophecy. End-time doctrine is never for curiosity alone. It is for holy readiness.

The insertion of this warning in the Armageddon context also reminds the church that while the nations gather in rebellion, the people of God must not sleep. The world's rulers move toward judgment even while thinking they are asserting autonomy. The saints must live in the opposite spirit—awake, clothed, and ready for the coming of the Lord.

Armageddon and the Hope of the Kingdom

Armageddon is terrible, but it is not the end of hope. It is the necessary overthrow of the present beastly order so that the kingdom administration of Christ may proceed openly. Revelation 19 does not end in battlefield imagery alone. It is followed by Revelation 20, where Satan is bound, the first-resurrection company reigns with Christ, and the thousand-year kingdom unfolds. Thus Armageddon must be read not only as judgment, but as transition. It is the end of the present age of mature anti-God dominion and the beginning of the next stage in the outworking of God's redemptive purpose.

This is consistent with Daniel 2, where the stone cut without hands strikes the image of the kingdoms, crushes it, and becomes a great mountain filling the whole earth (Dan. 2:34-35). The destruction of human kingdom-power is followed by the establishment of God's kingdom. Daniel 7 likewise moves from beastly dominion and persecution to heavenly judgment and the giving of the kingdom to the holy ones (Dan. 7:26-27). Armageddon is Revelation's climactic portrayal of that same transition. Beastly power is crushed; the reign of Christ follows.

Therefore, the faithful should not hear "Armageddon" merely as a word of terror. They should hear it as the certainty that the rebellious world order will not endure forever. The beast will not rule without end. Babylon will not remain. The kings of the earth will not retain their defiant autonomy. Christ will appear, judge, and reign.

The Certainty of Armageddon's Outcome

Scripture never presents Armageddon as uncertain in outcome. The kings gather, but not to triumph. The beast makes war, but not to win. The dragon energizes rebellion, but only within the limits of divine permission. The outcome is fixed before the battle is described. This is one reason Revelation can portray the event with such royal certainty. The Lamb is already the One who conquered through His sacrificial death and resurrection. He is already worthy to open the scroll. He is already Lord of lords and King of kings. Armageddon is the historical manifestation of a victory whose rightness and certainty are already established in heaven.

This also means believers should never speak as though evil might somehow prevail in the final confrontation. Scripture gives no room for such fear. Armageddon is not a desperate last stand by God against a nearly equal enemy. It is the crushing of rebellion by the enthroned Christ. The same Lord who speaks to the churches, opens the seals, and governs the judgments of Revelation now appears as warrior-king. Evil is exposed, gathered, and destroyed.

Living in the Light of Armageddon

The doctrine of Armageddon should shape the believer's view of the world. It reveals that the political powers of the earth, however impressive, are temporary and accountable. It reveals that anti-God alliances may grow global, but they are still doomed. It reveals that demonic deception does not create sovereign history; it operates only within the purposes God has decreed. It reveals that Christ's return is not symbolic moral influence, but public royal intervention in judgment. It reveals that the present world order is moving, not toward self-redemption, but toward divine reckoning.

This doctrine should also produce separation from the beastly spirit of the age. If the kings of the earth are being gathered for destruction, the people of God cannot place their hope in the permanence of the present order. If Babylon falls, believers must not admire her luxuries. If the beast is doomed, they must not fear him into compromise. If Christ comes as warrior-king, they must be awake and clothed, not spiritually asleep. Armageddon therefore calls the church away from worldly confidence and into steadfast loyalty to the Lamb.

It also strengthens courage. The final anti-God order may appear overwhelming. Revelation itself does not minimize its scope or aggression. Yet Armageddon declares that no beastly coalition can outlast the appearing of Christ. The holy ones may be pressed, but they are not abandoned. The kings may gather, but they gather to their own judgment. The present age may rage, but the Son will break the nations with a rod of iron. The doctrine of Armageddon therefore steadies the church. It reminds believers that the future belongs not to dragon, beast, false prophet, or Babylon, but to Jehovah and to His Christ.

Armageddon, then, is the final divinely appointed gathering of the kings of the rebellious world under demonic deception for the war of the great day of God the Almighty, culminating in the visible appearing of Christ, the destruction of the beast and false prophet, the slaughter of the gathered anti-God armies, and the overthrow of the present beastly order before the thousand-year reign. It is the Revelation form of the Day of Jehovah, the fulfillment of the prophetic pattern of gathered nations meeting divine judgment, and the necessary transition from the present anti-God age to the open kingdom administration of Christ. It is severe because rebellion is severe. It is certain because Christ reigns. And it is hopeful for the faithful because the battle does not end with chaos, but with the triumph of the Lamb who judges and wages war in righteousness.

CHAPTER 8 Explaining the "Rapture" in the Biblical Framework

The Need to Explain the "Rapture" Biblically

Few doctrines in modern prophetic teaching have been surrounded by more confusion than the so-called "rapture." In popular religious thought, the term often refers to a sudden disappearance of Christians from the earth, a secret coming of Christ prior to the Great Tribulation, and a removal of the church so that the world is left behind to face the final crisis alone. Yet when the relevant biblical passages are examined in their own context, this popular picture does not arise from the text itself. It is the product of a later prophetic system imposed upon Scripture, not the plain teaching of the prophets, Jesus, Paul, and Revelation.

The New Testament does speak of believers being gathered to Christ. It does speak of the dead in Christ being raised and of those belonging to Him sharing in His glory. It does speak of a catching up in relation to the Lord's coming. But these truths must be interpreted within the broader prophetic framework of Scripture. When Daniel, the Olivet Discourse, Paul's letters, and Revelation are read together through the historical-grammatical method, the biblical doctrine becomes much clearer than many assume. The so-called "rapture" is not a secret evacuation of all believers from the earth before the Great Tribulation. It is the resurrection and transformation of those called to heavenly rulership with Christ, taking place in direct relation to His presence and within the larger outworking of God's kingdom purpose.

This means the subject must be rescued from sensationalism and restored to biblical order. The issue is not whether believers are gathered to Christ. Scripture clearly teaches that they are. The issue is how that gathering occurs, whom it concerns, when it unfolds, and how it fits into the prophetic structure of the last days. The answer must come from Scripture itself, not from a system that divides Christ's coming into hidden and visible phases that the text does not support.

The Key Passage in First Thessalonians

The central passage usually cited in discussions of the rapture is 1 Thessalonians 4:13-18. Paul writes to comfort believers who were grieving over fellow Christians who had died. His concern is not to satisfy speculative curiosity about future events, but to correct sorrow shaped by misunderstanding. He says, "We do not want you to be ignorant concerning those who are sleeping in death, so that you may not sorrow just as the rest also do who have no hope" (1 Thess. 4:13). This opening is vital. The whole discussion is rooted in the doctrine of resurrection, not in a theory of mass disappearance.

Paul then explains, "Because if our faith is that Jesus died and rose again, so, too, those who have fallen asleep through Jesus God will bring with him" (1 Thess. 4:14). The analogy is clear. Just as Jesus truly died and was raised, so those who belong to Him and have died will also be raised. Paul's emphasis is not on a hidden removal from the earth while still living in the ordinary fleshly state. His emphasis is on resurrection hope. The dead in Christ are not forgotten, and those alive at the Lord's coming do not gain an advantage over them.

He continues, "For this is what we tell you by Jehovah's word, that we the living who survive to the presence of the Lord will in no way precede those who have fallen asleep in death; because the Lord himself will descend from heaven with a commanding call, with an archangel's voice and with God's trumpet, and those who are dead in union with Christ will rise first. Afterward we the living who are surviving will together with them be caught away in clouds to meet the Lord in the air, and thus we shall always be with the Lord" (1 Thess. 4:15-17). Several features of this passage immediately stand against the popular doctrine of a secret rapture.

First, the event is not secret. The Lord descends "with a commanding call," "with an archangel's voice," and "with God's trumpet." This is public, royal, and dramatic language. It belongs to divine manifestation, not hidden removal. Second, the dead in Christ are central. They "rise first." Therefore the passage is governed by resurrection. Third, the living are caught up "together with them," showing that the catching up is inseparable from the resurrection of those already asleep in death. Fourth, the purpose is to meet the Lord and remain with Him. Paul's concern is union with Christ, not escape into sensational prophetic scenarios.

The Greek verb often translated "caught up" is harpazō, meaning to seize, snatch, or catch away. It refers to decisive divine action. But the verb itself does not establish a secret disappearance theory. Its meaning must be determined by the context in which Paul uses it. Here the context is resurrection, transformation, and gathering to the openly descending Lord. The text does not say that the world continues normally while believers vanish invisibly. It presents a visible, audible, eschatological event bound to the Lord's coming.

The Gathering in Relation to Resurrection

Paul's fullest explanation of resurrection and transformation comes in 1 Corinthians 15. There he writes, "Flesh and blood cannot inherit God's kingdom, nor does corruption inherit incorruption" (1 Cor. 15:50). That single statement is decisive. If those called to heavenly life are to inherit the kingdom in its heavenly sense, they cannot do so in ordinary mortal flesh. A change is necessary. Paul continues, "Look! I tell you a sacred secret: We shall not all fall asleep in death, but we shall all be changed, in a moment, in the twinkling of an eye, during the last trumpet. For the trumpet will sound, and the dead will be raised up incorruptible, and we shall be changed" (1 Cor. 15:51-52).

This passage explains what 1 Thessalonians 4 requires. The gathering to Christ involves resurrection and transformation. It is not ordinary bodily relocation in a flesh-and-blood condition. The dead are raised incorruptible, and the living are changed. Paul adds, "For this which is corruptible must put on incorruption, and this which is mortal must put on immortality" (1 Cor. 15:53). The heavenly inheritance therefore belongs to those transformed by God. The so-called rapture cannot be separated from this resurrection-change. It is not a doctrine of fleshly transport to heaven before tribulation. It is the doctrine of God bringing His heavenly heirs into the state necessary for that calling.

The phrase "during the last trumpet" also matters. Paul's language again rules out the notion of a hidden secret phase before the visible end-time crisis. Trumpet imagery in Scripture belongs to divine assembly, intervention, warning, and kingdom significance. Jesus also speaks of a "great trumpet" when the chosen ones are gathered at His coming (Matt. 24:31). The parallels are too strong to ignore. Paul's teaching on resurrection and catching up stands in harmony with Jesus' public coming and gathering, not in contradiction to it.

The Presence of Christ and the Gathering of Believers

Paul places the gathering of believers in direct connection with the presence of Christ. In 2 Thessalonians 2:1-2 he writes, "Now concerning the presence of our Lord Jesus Christ and our being gathered together to him, we ask you, brothers, not to be quickly shaken." He then says that this day will not come unless the apostasy comes first and the man of lawlessness is revealed (2 Thess. 2:3). This text is devastating to the common secret-rapture system because it explicitly joins the gathering of believers to Christ with the same eschatological context in which the apostasy and the man of lawlessness appear.

If the gathering occurred in a secret pre-tribulation event, Paul's reasoning would collapse. Instead, his argument is that believers must not think the day has already arrived because certain identifiable prophetic developments must occur first. The gathering is therefore not detached from the final crisis. It belongs within it. The same Christ whose presence destroys the lawless one is the Christ to whom believers are gathered. There is no textual basis here for splitting the coming of Christ into a hidden phase for the church and a later visible phase for judgment. Paul knows of one great presence, one gathering, one final victory over the lawless order.

This harmonizes perfectly with Matthew 24. Jesus says that after the Great Tribulation, the Son of Man appears in heaven with power and great glory, and then "he will send out his angels with a great trumpet sound, and they will gather his chosen ones from the four winds" (Matt. 24:30-31). Again, the sequence is plain. Great Tribulation first, visible coming of Christ second, gathering of the chosen ones third. The text does not support a pre-tribulation removal of all believers from the earth. It places the gathering after the tribulation and at the visible manifestation of Christ.

Why the Secret Rapture Theory Fails

The secret rapture theory usually depends on separating passages that Scripture itself joins and joining passages that Scripture itself distinguishes. It takes 1 Thessalonians 4 and 1 Corinthians 15 as though they described a hidden preliminary event, then places that event before the Great Tribulation, even though neither passage says so. It then treats Matthew 24 and Revelation 19 as though they described an entirely different coming of Christ, even though the same themes of trumpet, gathering, visible manifestation, and judgment appear throughout.

The theory also often treats the church as absent from the final crisis by assumption rather than by text. But Jesus speaks of "the chosen ones" in direct relation to the Great Tribulation and says the days are cut short for their sake (Matt. 24:22). Revelation repeatedly speaks of the holy ones enduring under the beast's pressure (Rev. 13:7, 10; 14:12). Paul speaks of the apostasy and the man of lawlessness before the gathering. The biblical pattern consistently presents the people of God in the setting of the final conflict, not removed from it by a prior secret event.

Another weakness of the secret rapture theory is that it blurs the distinction between resurrection hope and escape theology. Paul's concern in 1 Thessalonians 4 is the resurrection of those who have fallen asleep in death. The comfort of the passage is that the dead in Christ are not left behind. If the text is turned into a dramatic theory about mass disappearance, the actual pastoral point is displaced. The chapter is about Christ's victory over death and the gathering of His people to Himself, not about a suspenseful prophetic disappearance scenario.

The Biblical Distinction Between Two Hopes

To explain the gathering to Christ properly, one must also preserve the biblical distinction between those called to reign with Christ in heaven and the broader body of the righteous who receive everlasting life under God's kingdom. Scripture does not present one flat future hope in which every faithful person receives the same role in exactly the same form. Revelation 20 speaks of those who reign with Christ for the thousand years, specifically those sharing in the first resurrection (Rev. 20:4-6). Revelation 5:9-10 speaks of those purchased for God who are made to be a kingdom and priests and who are to reign. Revelation 14 presents the one hundred forty-four thousand standing with the Lamb on Mount Zion, having His name and His Father's name written on their foreheads (Rev. 14:1). These passages together identify a distinct company associated with heavenly rulership.

This is why the so-called rapture must be interpreted specifically in relation to that heavenly calling. The catching up of 1 Thessalonians 4 and the transformation of 1 Corinthians 15 belong to those who inherit the kingdom in that heavenly sense and who must therefore be changed from corruption to incorruption. They are not texts about the worldwide disappearance of every faithful believer from the earth. Rather, they concern the completion of the body that will reign with Christ.

At the same time, Scripture also speaks of the righteous inheriting the earth, receiving everlasting life, and dwelling in the restored order under God's kingdom. Jesus says, "Happy are the mild-tempered, since they will inherit the earth" (Matt. 5:5). Psalm 37 repeatedly states that the righteous will possess the earth and reside forever upon it (Ps. 37:9, 11, 29). Revelation 21 presents a new heaven and a new earth with God dwelling with mankind. Therefore, the biblical picture includes both heavenly rulership with Christ and everlasting life for the righteous under that kingdom administration. The gathering described in the so-called rapture passages belongs specifically to the heavenly company.

The Progressive Gathering of the Heavenly Rulers

The biblical evidence points, not to one cinematic moment in which all chosen believers vanish from earth, but to the completion of a heavenly body selected across the Christian era and brought to its full number in connection with the time of the end. Jesus' apostles were among the earliest promised a role in His kingdom. He told them they would sit on thrones judging the twelve tribes of Israel (Matt. 19:28; Luke 22:28-30). Paul writes of faithful believers receiving a heavenly inheritance and sharing in Christ's reign. Revelation presents the sealing of the one hundred forty-four thousand, not as a random number, but as the completed totality of those appointed to that role (Rev. 7:1-8; 14:1-5).

Those who died in Christ during the Christian era did not ascend immediately to heaven in conscious life at death. Scripture consistently teaches that the dead are asleep in death, unconscious, awaiting God's resurrection act. Jesus spoke of Lazarus as sleeping before plainly saying that he had died (John 11:11-14). Ecclesiastes says the dead are conscious of nothing at all (Eccl. 9:5, 10). Paul repeatedly speaks of believers who have "fallen asleep in death," awaiting resurrection (1 Thess. 4:13-15; 1 Cor. 15:18, 20). Therefore, the heavenly heirs do not enter their inheritance immediately at death in a conscious disembodied condition. They remain asleep until raised by God.

The resurrection of these heavenly rulers begins in the time associated with Christ's presence. Those already dead are raised first. Those who remain alive during the closing period do not gain advantage over the dead, but when their earthly course is finished, they too are brought into that heavenly life by immediate transformation at death without prolonged waiting in the sleep of death. In that sense the gathering unfolds progressively under Christ's administration rather than as one theatrical removal from the planet. The key issue is completion of the heavenly ruling body, not the disappearance of all Christians from earthly life.

The Meaning of Meeting the Lord in the Air

Paul says believers are "caught away in clouds to meet the Lord in the air" (1 Thess. 4:17). This phrase has often been read in a crude physical way, as though believers rise bodily into the sky and remain suspended there. But Paul's language is eschatological and symbolic in the sense normal to apocalyptic and prophetic description. Clouds are repeatedly associated with divine presence and heavenly glory. Jesus comes with the clouds (Matt. 24:30; Rev. 1:7). The Son of Man in Daniel comes with the clouds of heaven (Dan. 7:13). Meeting the Lord "in the air" therefore signifies being gathered into His sphere of heavenly dominion and presence, not necessarily a prolonged visual spectacle in the atmosphere for the world to observe.

The word "meet" itself can carry the sense of going out to meet a dignitary and then accompanying him. In any case, the controlling point is that believers are united with Christ at His coming. Paul's purpose is not to satisfy curiosity about atmospheric mechanics. He is emphasizing that those in Christ, whether dead or living at the time, will not be separated from Him. "And thus we shall always be with the Lord" (1 Thess. 4:17). That is the heart of the comfort.

This also fits the larger biblical pattern. Christ is openly manifested in glory, His people are gathered to Him, and the kingdom advances. The text does not require a theory of secret removal years before the public crisis. It requires reunion with Christ in the context of resurrection and transformation.

The "Rapture" and the Great Tribulation

One of the most important questions is whether the gathering to Christ occurs before the Great Tribulation in a secret event or in relation to Christ's public presence after that tribulation. Scripture consistently supports the latter. Jesus says, "Immediately after the tribulation of those days" the heavenly signs occur, the Son of Man appears, and the chosen ones are gathered (Matt. 24:29-31). Paul says the gathering to Christ is connected to the day that cannot come until the apostasy and the revelation of the man of lawlessness (2 Thess. 2:1-3). Revelation shows the holy ones enduring under beastly opposition and the great crowd coming out of the Great Tribulation (Rev. 7:14; 13:7, 10; 14:12).

This means the biblical framework does not support a pre-tribulation worldwide removal of Christians from the earth. The people of God are present in the setting of the final crisis. Their faithfulness is tested under pressure. Their vindication comes with the appearing of Christ, not with an earlier secret disappearance. The heavenly rulers are gathered to Christ in connection with His presence, but that gathering belongs within the prophetic sequence that includes the apostasy, the lawless one, the beastly order, and the Great Tribulation.

This point must be stressed because the escape model of prophecy often weakens the church's readiness for endurance. If believers are taught that they will be removed before the final crisis, they may misunderstand the repeated biblical calls to steadfastness under persecution and deception. Scripture instead prepares the church to remain faithful through whatever God appoints, under the assurance that Christ will gather His own, destroy the lawless order, and vindicate the holy ones at His appearing.

The One Hundred Forty-Four Thousand and the Heavenly Calling

Revelation 7 and 14 provide important light for understanding the gathering to Christ in the heavenly sense. Revelation 7 presents one hundred forty-four thousand sealed from the tribes of the sons of Israel before the vision shifts to the great crowd from all nations. Revelation 14 then shows the one hundred forty-four thousand with the Lamb on Mount Zion, having His name and His Father's name on their foreheads, singing a new song before the throne, and being described as purchased from among mankind as firstfruits to God and to the Lamb (Rev. 14:1-4). Their identity is bound to the Lamb's heavenly rule and to a distinct status in relation to God's purpose.

The number symbolizes the complete totality of those chosen for this priestly and royal role. Revelation 20 clarifies that those sharing in the first resurrection reign with Christ for the thousand years and serve as priests of God and of the Christ (Rev. 20:4-6). The gathering described by Paul in 1 Thessalonians 4 fits naturally with this company. They are the ones transformed from mortality to incorruption for heavenly kingdom service. The catching up is therefore not the removal of all righteous mankind from earth, but the completion of the body appointed to reign with Christ in heaven.

This preserves the wider biblical pattern. Christ does not leave the earth forever empty of faithful human life. Rather, He gathers His heavenly co-rulers while also establishing the kingdom administration under which the righteous inherit life in the restored order. The heavenly and earthly dimensions of hope must not be confused.

The Error of Treating Death as Immediate Heavenly Life

Many errors about the so-called rapture are connected to a deeper error about death. If one assumes that the faithful dead are already alive in heaven consciously enjoying their reward, then resurrection becomes little more than an accessory doctrine, and passages like 1 Thessalonians 4 lose their actual force. But Scripture does not teach that the dead in Christ are already living consciously in heaven before resurrection. Paul says they are "sleeping in death." He says the dead in Christ "will rise first." If they were already alive in heaven in the fullness of their reward, Paul's language would become confusing and unnecessary.

The biblical doctrine is that death is real cessation of personal life until God restores life by resurrection. This is why resurrection is hope. Jesus says, "I am the resurrection and the life" (John 11:25). Paul says if the dead are not raised, then even those who have fallen asleep in union with Christ have perished (1 Cor. 15:18). The power of 1 Thessalonians 4 rests precisely here: those who died are not lost, and the living do not outrun them. God will raise them and gather them to Christ. The so-called rapture is therefore a resurrection doctrine, not an escape-from-death doctrine.

The Biblical Framework of the Gathering

When the relevant passages are allowed to stand together, a coherent structure emerges. Christ ascended to heaven and has progressively selected those called to reign with Him. Faithful members of this heavenly calling who died remained asleep in death, awaiting resurrection. In the time associated with Christ's presence, the dead in Christ are raised first. The remaining members of that heavenly body are brought into the same glorified condition as they complete their earthly course. This gathering belongs to the public presence of Christ, to the final defeat of the lawless and beastly order, and to the completion of the body that will reign with Him during the thousand years.

This understanding preserves the plain sense of Paul's words, the sequence of Matthew 24, and the order of Revelation 19–20. It also prevents the common errors of imagining an invisible pre-tribulation removal of all Christians, of confusing resurrection with innate immortality, and of erasing the biblical distinction between heavenly rulers and the broader righteous who receive everlasting life under God's kingdom.

The Comfort of the Biblical Doctrine

Paul closes his teaching in 1 Thessalonians 4 by saying, "Keep comforting one another with these words" (1 Thess. 4:18). That pastoral purpose must remain central. The doctrine of gathering to Christ is not meant to produce anxiety, sensationalism, or prophetic vanity. It is meant to comfort believers with the certainty that death does not separate them permanently from Christ, that those who belong to Him will be raised, and that the living faithful will not lose their place in His kingdom purpose. The comfort lies in Christ's victory over death and in the certainty of union with Him.

This comfort is actually deepened, not weakened, when the doctrine is placed in its biblical framework. The church need not rely on an invented system of secret escape to have hope. Its hope is anchored in something far greater: the public triumph of Christ, the resurrection of the dead, the gathering of His heavenly co-rulers, the vindication of the faithful, the destruction of the anti-God order, and the establishment of His kingdom administration over the earth. The gathering to Christ is not less glorious because it is not a secret rapture. It is more glorious because it belongs to the openly manifested reign of the risen Lord.

Explaining the "Rapture" Within the Whole Counsel of God

The so-called "rapture," then, must be explained within the whole counsel of God and not through later prophetic speculation. Scripture does teach a decisive gathering of believers to Christ. It does teach a catching up. It does teach resurrection and transformation. But it teaches these things in direct relation to Christ's presence, to the resurrection of the dead in Christ, to the final prophetic crisis, and to the completion of those called to reign with Him. It does not teach a secret, pre-tribulation disappearance of all believers from the earth.

The biblical doctrine is richer and more coherent than the popular system. It preserves the resurrection hope, honors the order of prophecy, keeps the Great Tribulation in its proper place, and upholds the distinction between the heavenly calling and the earthly inheritance under God's kingdom. Above all, it keeps Christ Himself at the center. The church's hope is not in escaping the world through a hidden event. Its hope is in the appearing of Jesus Christ, who will raise His own, gather them to Himself, destroy the lawless and beastly order, and bring God's kingdom purpose into its next openly manifested stage.

For that reason, the faithful should not cling to a dramatic theory because it is familiar or emotionally attractive. They should cling to what Scripture actually says. The dead in Christ will rise first. Those belonging to His heavenly kingdom will be transformed. They will be caught up together with the resurrected ones to meet the Lord. The apostasy and lawless rebellion will not prevent His purpose. The Great Tribulation will not overturn His decree. Armageddon will not threaten His victory. The Lamb will reign, His heavenly co-rulers will be complete, and God's kingdom will advance in full authority over the earth. That is the biblical framework of the so-called rapture, and within that framework the doctrine becomes not a source of confusion, but a source of deep and steady hope.

CHAPTER 9 Explaining Death

Death in the Biblical Worldview

Death is one of the most universal realities in human experience and one of the most misunderstood subjects in religion. Men know that death comes, yet they have produced many conflicting theories to soften its meaning, deny its finality, or transfer the dead into some other mode of conscious existence. Some say the dead immediately ascend to heavenly joy. Others say the dead descend into torment. Still others imagine an immortal soul released from the body, continuing its awareness in another realm while awaiting reunion with the body later. The Bible presents a far more consistent and sober doctrine. Death is the cessation of life. It is the end of conscious human activity. It is the return of the person to the state from which he was formed, awaiting only the possibility of future life through the resurrection power of God.

The importance of this doctrine cannot be overstated. If death is misunderstood, then resurrection is misunderstood. If the soul is misunderstood, then judgment, hope, and the future kingdom are also distorted. Much confusion in theology comes from importing philosophical ideas into Scripture rather than allowing Scripture to define its own terms. The Bible's teaching is simple, consistent, and closely tied to its doctrine of creation. Man is not presented as a body housing an immortal soul that naturally survives death. Man is presented as a living soul. Therefore when man dies, the soul dies. The future hope is not the soul's escape from the body but God's act of restoring life through resurrection.

This biblical teaching begins in Genesis, continues through the Law, the Prophets, the Psalms, the Gospels, the apostolic letters, and Revelation, and remains entirely consistent when read according to the historical-grammatical meaning of the words used. Because death stands near the center of every doctrine of last things, it must be explained first according to the Bible itself and not according to human tradition. Only then can one properly understand the resurrection hope, the final judgment, the second death, and the new creation in which death is finally abolished.

Man Did Not Receive a Soul but Became a Soul

The foundational text for the biblical doctrine of death is Genesis 2:7: "And Jehovah God proceeded to form the man out of dust from the ground and to blow into his nostrils the breath of life, and the man came to be a living soul." This verse is decisive because it does not say that the man received an immortal soul as a separate conscious entity. It says the man came to be a living soul. The soul in this first creation statement is the whole living person.

This language sets the pattern for all later biblical usage. The Hebrew word ne′phesh, commonly translated "soul," regularly refers to the living creature itself, the whole individual. Adam was not given a soul as though he were one thing and the soul another. He became a soul when the formed body was animated by the breath of life from

God. Dust plus breath produced a living soul. When those elements separate in death, the soul ceases as a living person. The verse is therefore not only a creation text. It is also the key that explains death.

This understanding is confirmed repeatedly in Scripture. Leviticus 5:1 speaks of "a soul" who sins. Leviticus 23:30 speaks of "any soul" doing work. Deuteronomy 24:7 speaks of kidnapping "a soul," clearly meaning a person. Job says, "How long will you men keep irritating my soul?" (Job 19:2). Psalm 119:28 says, "My soul has been sleepless from grief." In each of these passages, "soul" refers to the person, not to an invisible and independently conscious entity inside the person. The Bible's usage is concrete and direct. The soul is the living being.

The Greek word psy·khe′ in the Christian Greek Scriptures follows the same pattern. Jesus says, "My soul is troubled" (John 12:27), referring to Himself as a person. Acts 2:43 says fear came upon "every soul," meaning every person. Romans 13:1 says, "Let every soul be in subjection to the superior authorities," again meaning every individual. First Peter 3:20 says that "eight souls" were carried safely through the water, meaning eight persons. The language is simple and consistent. A soul is a living creature, a living person, not a naturally immortal conscious essence separable from the body in ordinary biblical thought.

This point alone overturns much traditional confusion. If man is a soul, then death must be understood as the death of the person, not the release of one part into true life while another part perishes. The biblical doctrine of death begins with the biblical doctrine of man.

The Soul Can Die

Because the soul in Scripture refers to the living person, the Bible can speak naturally of the soul dying. Ezekiel 18:4 states, "The soul that is sinning—it itself will die." That sentence is utterly plain. It does not say the body dies while the soul continues in conscious existence. It says the soul dies. The meaning fits the entire context of Ezekiel's argument about personal responsibility before God. The individual who sins is the one who dies.

The Law speaks similarly. Numbers 6:6 refers to "a dead soul," meaning a dead person or corpse. Leviticus 21:1 uses the same kind of expression. These passages would be unintelligible if the biblical writers assumed that the true self was an immortal soul living consciously elsewhere while only the body lay dead. Scripture is not confused. The soul that lived is now dead. That is the point.

The same usage appears in narrative and prayer. Elijah asks "that his soul might die" (1 Ki. 19:4). Jonah repeats that his soul should die because he sees death as the end of his conscious earthly life (Jonah 4:8). Jesus speaks of "to kill a soul" in the sense of putting a person to death (Mark 3:4). The language is neither symbolic nor imprecise. It reflects the Bible's stable anthropology. A soul is a living creature. When the creature dies, the soul dies.

This does not mean Scripture denies future hope. It means future hope cannot be grounded in natural human immortality. If the soul can die, then immortality is not man's native possession. Future life must come by divine gift. This is exactly what the Bible teaches. Eternal life is the gift of God through Jesus Christ (Rom. 6:23). Resurrection is the answer to death because death is real. If man were naturally immortal in his soul, resurrection would lose its central place. But the Bible makes resurrection essential precisely because death means the cessation of life and consciousness until God acts to restore it.

The Penalty Announced in Eden

The clearest statement of death's meaning comes in God's sentence upon Adam. Genesis 3:19 says, "For dust you are and to dust you will return." The punishment was not transfer to another sphere of conscious experience. It was death. Adam had been formed from the dust. By sin he forfeited life, and his end would be return to the dust. There is no suggestion in the text that an immortal element within Adam would continue living in another realm while only his body returned to dust. The sentence is complete, direct, and coherent with Genesis 2:7. The living soul formed from dust and animated by God's life-breath would die and return to the ground.

This sentence also sets the pattern for the biblical doctrine of death thereafter. Death is the undoing of creaturely life. It is not annihilation of all hope, because God may still raise the dead. But it is the real end of present life. This is why Scripture can speak of death as an enemy (1 Cor. 15:26). It is not man's natural friend or doorway to fuller consciousness. It is the wages of sin, a curse upon the race through Adam's transgression (Rom. 5:12). Only by understanding death this way can one grasp the full glory of Christ's victory over it.

The Dead Are Unconscious

The Bible repeatedly teaches that the dead are unconscious. Ecclesiastes 9:5 says, "The living are conscious that they will die; but as for the dead, they are conscious of nothing at all." Verse 10 adds, "There is no work nor devising nor knowledge nor wisdom in Sheol, the place to which you are going." These statements are direct and should not be explained away. Death is not a heightened state of awareness. The dead know nothing. Their activity, planning, knowledge, and wisdom have ceased.

Psalm 146:4 says of dying man, "His spirit goes out, he goes back to his ground; in that day his thoughts do perish." Again the meaning is not obscure. Death ends the person's earthly consciousness. The thoughts do not migrate into another conscious mode. They perish. Psalm 115:17 says, "The dead themselves do not praise Jah, nor do any going down into the silence." If the dead were consciously enjoying heaven immediately, such language would be deeply misleading. But it is not misleading. The dead are silent because death is a state of unconsciousness.

This same truth appears in the language Jesus uses about death. When Lazarus died, Jesus said, "Lazarus our friend has fallen asleep, but I am traveling there to awaken him from sleep" (John 11:11). He later spoke plainly and said Lazarus had died (John 11:14). Jesus' use of sleep as a figure for death is meaningful because sleep conveys unconsciousness, inactivity, and the possibility of awakening by divine power. He does not speak of Lazarus as living consciously in heaven or in torment. He speaks of him as asleep in death, awaiting resurrection. Martha's words confirm this when she says, "I know he will rise in the resurrection on the last day" (John 11:24). The family's hope was not that Lazarus was already alive elsewhere. Their hope was future resurrection.

Paul uses the same language repeatedly. He speaks of Christians who have "fallen asleep in death" (1 Thess. 4:13-15; 1 Cor. 15:18, 20). The image is not mere sentiment. It reflects the biblical reality that the dead are not active, conscious participants in heavenly life while awaiting reunion with the body. They are asleep in death until God awakens them by resurrection. This is why the resurrection is necessary, not ornamental.

Rachel's Soul Going Out

Some appeal to Genesis 35:18, which says of Rachel, "As her soul was going out (because she died), she called his name Benoni." Yet this passage does not teach that Rachel's soul was an immortal conscious being departing to continue life elsewhere. The text itself explains the phrase by saying "because she died." Her "soul" here refers to her life, her living existence ebbing away. This usage is entirely normal within the Bible's own definitions. As already seen, soul can refer either to the person as a living creature or to the life enjoyed by that creature. When Rachel's soul "went out," her life departed. That is why she died.

Other passages use the same language. Elijah prayed, and the widow's son's "soul came back within him and he came to life" (1 Ki. 17:22). The point is not that a conscious disembodied being returned from another realm after conversation in heaven or torment in hell. The point is that life returned, and the child revived. The Bible can speak of soul in this extended sense without abandoning its fundamental meaning. Life departs; life returns. The person dies; the person lives again. The language is consistent when read on biblical terms.

The Meaning of Spirit in Relation to Death

Another major source of confusion is the Bible's use of the word spirit. Psalm 146:4 says man's spirit goes out. Ecclesiastes 12:7 says,

"Then the dust returns to the earth just as it happened to be and the spirit itself returns to the true God who gave it." These verses are sometimes taken to mean that a conscious disembodied self ascends to God at death. But the biblical meaning of spirit does not support that conclusion.

The Hebrew word ru′ach and the Greek word pneu′ma basically carry the sense of breath, wind, or the animating force of life depending on context. In relation to living creatures, spirit can refer to the life-force by which the organism lives. Genesis 7:22, describing the Flood, says that all in whose nostrils "the breath of the force of life" was active died. Psalm 104:29 says that when God takes away their spirit, creatures expire and return to their dust. Thus spirit in these passages is not a separately conscious being. It is the life-force or life-breath by which the creature lives.

This is why Ecclesiastes 12:7 says the spirit returns to God who gave it. The life-force is no longer active in the body. The person has died. All hope of future life now rests with God, because He is the giver and restorer of life. The spirit does not return to God as a consciously functioning mini-person. It returns in the sense that the life once granted now lies wholly in God's hands if it is ever to be restored. The body goes back to dust; the life-force belongs to the Creator; the person is dead. Only resurrection can reunite life with the person in conscious existence again.

An illustration is helpful. Electricity animates a machine so that it functions. When the current stops, the machine ceases to function. The current has not become the machine's personality living elsewhere. In a limited and imperfect sense, the relation of spirit to the body is similar. Spirit animates the creature. When that spirit is removed, the creature dies. The spirit does not continue as the conscious person independent of the body. The person is dead.

Death and the End of Human Activity

Scripture consistently connects death with inactivity. The dead do not praise, plan, think, or work. They are silent in the grave. Job says, "The man must die and lie powerless; and an earthling man must expire, and where is he?" (Job 14:10). He compares death to a man lying down and not getting up "until the heavens are no more" (Job 14:12). Yet in the same chapter Job expresses hope that God would call and he would answer, pointing to resurrection (Job 14:13-15). Death is therefore inactivity and unconsciousness, but not hopelessness if God purposes to raise.

This doctrine also explains why the Bible can speak of graves, memorial tombs, and Sheol or Hades as the state of the dead. Sheol in the Hebrew Scriptures and Hades in the Greek Scriptures denote the grave, the realm of death, the condition of the dead, not a place of conscious torment or separate active existence for the faithful. Jacob said he would go down to Sheol mourning for Joseph (Gen. 37:35). Job wanted to be hidden in Sheol until God's anger passed (Job 14:13). Jesus was said not to be left in Hades, because He was raised from death (Acts 2:27, 31). The consistent biblical pattern is that death places men in the grave, the realm of unconsciousness, from which only resurrection delivers them.

The Contrast Between Death and Resurrection

Because death is real cessation of life, resurrection becomes absolutely central. Scripture does not portray resurrection as reunion of an already-living immortal soul with a new body. It portrays resurrection as God's act of restoring life to those who have died. Jesus says, "The hour is coming in which all those in the memorial tombs will hear his voice and come out" (John 5:28-29). Those in the memorial tombs are not living consciously in heaven or hell in the passage. They are in the tombs, and Christ's voice brings them out through resurrection.

Paul makes the same point in 1 Corinthians 15. If there is no resurrection, then those who have fallen asleep in Christ have perished (1 Cor. 15:18). That statement only makes sense if the dead are truly dead. If they were already consciously living in blessedness, Paul could not say they had perished if there were no resurrection. His argument depends on death being real cessation and resurrection being real restoration. Christ's resurrection is "the firstfruits of those who have fallen asleep in death" (1 Cor. 15:20), proving both the reality of death and the certainty of future restoration by God's power.

This also explains why Jesus' own death was genuine. He did not merely shed a body while His true self continued living in another form without interruption. He "poured out his soul to death" (Isa. 53:12). He gave His life as a ransom in exchange for many (Matt. 20:28). He was dead, and God raised Him on the third day. The power and glory of the resurrection depend on the reality of death. If death were only a doorway to higher consciousness, the biblical emphasis on God raising the dead would be strangely overstated. But because death truly ends human life and consciousness, resurrection is the mighty act by which God conquers death and restores what man lost through sin.

Death as an Enemy

Scripture calls death an enemy. First Corinthians 15:26 says, "As the last enemy, death is to be brought to nothing." This single description is profoundly revealing. Death is not presented as man's friend, natural transition, or doorway to immediate fulfillment. It is an enemy introduced through sin. Romans 5:12 says, "Through one man sin entered into the world and death through sin, and so death spread to all men because they had all sinned." Death is judicial in origin. It entered human experience through Adam's disobedience and spread through the race under sin.

That is why the Christian hope cannot be placed in death itself. The hope is not that death accomplishes for the faithful what resurrection later confirms. The hope is that Christ, who died and rose, will abolish death by raising the dead and finally removing death from God's creation. Revelation 20 says death and Hades are hurled into the lake of fire, identified as the second death (Rev. 20:14). Revelation 21 then says, "Death will be no more" (Rev. 21:4). These passages would make little sense if death were secretly a blessing and true life for the righteous. Scripture instead treats death as the great enemy that Christ defeats.

This is entirely coherent with the doctrine already established. Death is the cessation of life, the silence of the grave, the end of human thought and activity. Therefore it is rightly called an enemy. And because it is an enemy, the gospel promise is not centered on death but on resurrection and kingdom life.

The Error of the Immortal Soul Doctrine

The doctrine that man possesses an inherently immortal soul that survives death consciously is not the teaching of Scripture. It arises from philosophy and tradition, not from the biblical use of soul, spirit, death, and resurrection. Even where many religious teachers claim biblical support, the actual language of the Bible remains against them. Man became a living soul. The soul can die. The dead know nothing. The dead do not praise God. Their thoughts perish. Spirit returns to God in the sense that life rests with Him alone. Resurrection is necessary because the dead are truly dead.

This error causes many other errors. If the soul is thought to be naturally immortal, then eternal life is no longer seen as a gift but as a natural possession. If the dead are already fully conscious elsewhere, resurrection is diminished. If death is not really death, then the warning of second death in Revelation becomes confused. If the faithful dead are already living in fullness, then the urgency of Christ's future resurrection work becomes less central. Thus the immortal-soul doctrine does not merely add one incorrect detail. It distorts the whole framework of biblical eschatology.

The biblical doctrine is better, clearer, and more God-centered. Man does not possess immortality by nature. God alone has immortality in Himself in the absolute sense and grants endless life according to His purpose (1 Tim. 6:16). Eternal life is God's gift through Christ. Immortality for those called to heavenly reign is bestowed at resurrection and transformation (1 Cor. 15:53-54). Everlasting life for the righteous under God's kingdom is likewise a divine gift, not a natural human possession. This preserves all glory to God and all hope in Christ.

Death and the Sleep of the Dead

The Bible's repeated language of sleep is one of the most important and comforting ways it describes death. Sleep suggests unconsciousness, stillness, and the possibility of awakening. When Jesus said Lazarus had fallen asleep, He was not denying the seriousness of death. He was teaching that death for the one whom God will raise is like sleep in relation to God's power. Daniel 12:2 says, "Many of those asleep in the dust of the earth will wake up." The image is exact and beautiful. The dead are not portrayed as living consciously elsewhere. They are asleep in the dust until God awakens them.

Paul likewise says, "We do not want you to be ignorant concerning those who are sleeping in death" (1 Thess. 4:13). He then explains that the dead in Christ will rise first (1 Thess. 4:16). The comfort lies in the certainty that sleep will end when Christ calls. But until that awakening, death remains sleep, not active consciousness. This imagery also matches what men observe. The dead are still, silent, unresponsive, inactive. Scripture interprets this reality truthfully and gives hope beyond it.

Death and the Future Hope of the Righteous

The righteous do not need the doctrine of an immortal soul to have hope. Their hope is stronger because it rests on the promises of God, the resurrection of Christ, and the certainty of the kingdom. Jesus said, "I am the resurrection and the life. He that exercises faith in me, even though he dies, will come to life" (John 11:25). The hope is not that death is unreal. It is that Christ overcomes death. Paul says that Christ must reign until He has put all enemies under His feet, and the last enemy to be abolished is death (1 Cor. 15:25-26). The righteous therefore look beyond death to resurrection and kingdom life.

This also keeps death in its proper place. Believers need not fear death as ultimate, but neither must they romanticize it. It is a defeated enemy, yet still an enemy until God's purpose is complete. Christians grieve, but not as those who have no hope (1 Thess. 4:13). They may bury their dead with tears, but also with confidence that those asleep in Christ will rise. The dead are not now in perfect conscious bliss according to biblical language. They are resting in death until God remembers them and restores life.

The Hope Set Against Death

The Bible's answer to death is not philosophical speculation but divine action. God formed man from dust and gave him life. Man sinned and returned to dust. The dead are unconscious in the grave. The soul dies. The spirit or life-force returns to God, who alone can restore it. Christ died and was raised, becoming the firstfruits of those asleep in death. Therefore the dead will hear His voice and come out in the resurrection, some to life and some to judgment. The final enemy, death, will be abolished. In the new heaven and new earth, death will be no more.

This is the biblical doctrine in its full force and beauty. Death is real. It is the end of human conscious life. It is the enemy brought by sin. It is not the liberation of an immortal soul. It is not conscious transition to another realm. It is sleep in the dust, silence in the grave, return to the state of death from which only God can awaken man again. And because that is true, resurrection is glorious, Christ's triumph is meaningful, and the promise of everlasting life under God's kingdom shines with all the more power.

To explain death biblically, then, is to say plainly what Scripture says: man is a soul, the soul dies, the dead are unconscious, spirit is the life-force returning to God's care, and all hope beyond death depends wholly on the resurrection power of Jehovah through Jesus Christ. Only when death is understood in this way can one rightly understand the resurrection hope, the final judgment, the second death, and the new creation where tears are wiped away because death itself has finally been removed forever.

CHAPTER 10 Explaining Hell According to the Bible

The Need to Explain Hell Biblically

Few doctrines have produced more fear, confusion, and distortion than the doctrine of hell. In much traditional religion, hell is imagined as a place of conscious fiery torment where the wicked suffer forever without relief, without end, and without possibility of release. This view has been repeated so often that many assume it is plainly biblical. Yet when the words of Scripture are examined carefully in their own historical and grammatical setting, a very different picture emerges. The Bible does speak of death, the grave, destruction, judgment, and the final punishment of the wicked. But it does not teach that human beings possess an immortal soul that survives death in conscious torment in a fiery underworld.

This is not a minor correction. The doctrine of hell affects the whole structure of biblical truth. It affects the meaning of death, the necessity of resurrection, the justice of God, the nature of final judgment, and the hope set before the righteous. If hell is misunderstood, then the Bible's teaching on the grave, on the second death, and on eternal destruction is also distorted. The issue, therefore, is not whether there is judgment for the wicked. Scripture is severe and clear on that point. The issue is what Scripture actually means by the words often translated "hell" and what sort of final punishment God has revealed.

The Bible's teaching is far more consistent than the traditional doctrine of eternal torment. The Hebrew and Greek terms involved do not all mean the same thing, and confusion has often arisen because different original words were gathered under the single English term "hell." In some contexts the word refers to the common grave of mankind. In another it refers to the final destruction of the wicked. In another it refers to the abased condition of evil spirits. If these terms are blended together carelessly, serious doctrinal error follows. But if each term is allowed to keep its own meaning, the biblical doctrine becomes clear, solemn, and coherent.

Sheol and Hades: The Grave of Mankind

The most common biblical words later translated as "hell" in older English versions are the Hebrew Sheol and the Greek Hades. These terms fundamentally refer to the grave, the realm of the dead, or the condition of death. They do not in themselves mean a place of fiery conscious torment. Their use in Scripture proves this repeatedly.

Jacob, a faithful patriarch, said concerning his son Joseph, "I shall go down mourning to my son into Sheol" (Gen. 37:35). Jacob was not speaking of descending into a place of punishment. He meant that he himself would die and go to the grave. Job, another righteous man, prayed, "O that in Sheol you would conceal me, that you would hide me until your anger turns back, that you would set a limit for me and remember me!" (Job 14:13). Job did not view Sheol as a place of torment. He viewed it as the place of the dead where he longed to rest until God would remember him in resurrection. These passages alone should make the point plain. If Sheol were a place of fiery torment, the righteous could not speak of going there for relief.

The same is true in the Christian Greek Scriptures. At Pentecost Peter applied Psalm 16 to Jesus and said that His soul was not abandoned in Hades, nor did His flesh see corruption (Acts 2:27, 31). This means Jesus went to Hades when He died. But Jesus certainly did not go to a place of torment. He died and was in the grave until Jehovah raised Him. Therefore Hades, like Sheol, refers to the realm of the dead, the condition of death, and the grave from which resurrection is possible.

Revelation confirms this understanding. It says, "Death and Hades gave up the dead in them" (Rev. 20:13). Then it says, "Death and Hades were hurled into the lake of fire. This means the second death, the lake of fire" (Rev. 20:14). If Hades were a place of eternal torment, it could not itself be emptied and destroyed. But Revelation shows that Hades contains the dead and is later abolished. This fits perfectly with the biblical teaching that Hades is the grave and that death itself will one day be no more.

The Condition of Those in the Grave

If Sheol and Hades mean the grave, what is the condition of those who are there? Scripture answers with direct clarity. Ecclesiastes 9:5 says, "The living are conscious that they will die; but as for the dead, they are conscious of nothing at all." Verse 10 adds, "There is no work nor devising nor knowledge nor wisdom in Sheol, the place to which you are going." The dead are not described as aware, active, suffering, praising, planning, or remembering. They are unconscious.

Psalm 146:4 says of man, "His spirit goes out, he goes back to his ground; in that day his thoughts do perish." Psalm 115:17 says, "The dead themselves do not praise Jah, nor do any going down into the silence." If the dead were in conscious fiery torment, or even in conscious heavenly bliss, these statements would be impossible as written. But they are not impossible. They are true because death is the cessation of conscious life. The grave is silent. The dead know nothing. Their thoughts perish. Their activity ceases.

This is why Jesus could speak of death as sleep. When Lazarus died, Jesus said, "Lazarus our friend has fallen asleep, but I am traveling there to awaken him" (John 11:11). He later said plainly that Lazarus had died (John 11:14). The image of sleep is not sentimental decoration. It expresses the biblical reality that the dead are unconscious and await awakening by resurrection. If Lazarus had been consciously enjoying heaven or suffering elsewhere, Jesus' language would not fit the truth of his condition. But Jesus knew exactly what death was, and He described it as sleep until resurrection.

Paul uses the same language when speaking of believers who had "fallen asleep in death" (1 Cor. 15:18; 1 Thess. 4:13-15). Again, the point is that the dead are not already enjoying the fullness of their reward or enduring their punishment consciously somewhere else. They are asleep in death until God raises them. This makes resurrection necessary and glorious. If the dead were already fully alive in another realm, resurrection would lose its place as the great act of hope and victory over death.

Death, Not Torment, Is the Penalty for Sin

The biblical doctrine of hell must also be anchored in the original sentence against sin. Jehovah warned Adam, "In the day you eat from it you will positively die" (Gen. 2:17). After Adam sinned, God explained the sentence: "Dust you are and to dust you will return" (Gen. 3:19). The penalty was death, not eternal torment. Adam was formed from dust and would return to dust. No statement in the Eden narrative suggests that Adam would survive as an immortal soul in conscious punishment. The sentence was straightforward and consistent with man's creaturely nature. He would die.

The New Testament confirms the same truth. "The wages sin pays is death," not endless torment (Rom. 6:23). Paul adds, "The one who has died has been acquitted from his sin" (Rom. 6:7). This means death itself is the full wage paid by sin under Adamic condemnation. Scripture never says that death is merely the beginning of another endless penalty in fire for all the wicked in the popular sense. Rather, death is the penalty, and from that penalty only God can rescue by resurrection if He chooses.

This has profound theological significance. It shows that the common doctrine of eternal torment goes beyond what God stated as the sentence for sin. It also conflicts with the Bible's teaching that death is the enemy to be abolished, not the gateway to unending conscious torment for the mass of humanity. The gravity of sin is not lessened by saying its wage is death. On the contrary, death is dreadful precisely because it ends conscious life and leaves man with no hope except what God may grant through redemption and resurrection.

Gehenna: The Symbol of Final Destruction

A different term must now be distinguished from Sheol and Hades. Jesus often used the word Gehenna. This is not simply another synonym for the grave. Gehenna represents final, irreversible destruction under divine judgment. It does not mean conscious eternal torment, but it also does not refer to the common grave from which resurrection occurs. It points to the end of all hope for those judged wicked beyond remedy.

Gehenna derives from the Valley of Hinnom near Jerusalem, a place associated in Israel's history with defilement and abomination, including child sacrifice under apostate worship (2 Ki. 23:10; Jer. 7:31-32). In later Jewish memory it became a fitting symbol of divine rejection and destruction. When Jesus used Gehenna, He employed that known image to speak of ultimate ruin. He warned that one could be cast into Gehenna with body and soul destroyed (Matt. 10:28). He said it was better to lose an eye or hand than to be thrown into Gehenna (Matt. 5:29-30; 18:8-9). The stress in these warnings falls on destruction, loss, exclusion, and final judgment.

This becomes especially clear in Matthew 10:28, where Jesus says, "Do not become fearful of those who kill the body but cannot kill the soul; rather, fear him who can destroy both soul and body in Gehenna." The point is not torment but destruction. Men may kill the present life, but only God can bring complete and final destruction in judgment. Gehenna is therefore the symbol of irreversible loss of life before God, not eternal conscious suffering in flames.

This also harmonizes with the wider biblical language about the end of the wicked. Psalm 37 repeatedly says the wicked will be cut off, vanish, and be no more. Psalm 145:20 says, "Jehovah guards all those who love him, but all the wicked he will annihilate." Jesus speaks of broad road leading to destruction (Matt. 7:13). Paul speaks of everlasting destruction from the presence of the Lord (2 Thess. 1:9). Revelation calls the final judicial end "the second death" (Rev. 20:14; 21:8). These expressions do not naturally describe endless conscious torment. They describe destruction, annihilation, and death in their full judicial force.

Tartarus and the Demons

A third term often mixed into the doctrine of hell is Tartarus, used in verb form in 2 Peter 2:4. Peter says that God "did not hold back from punishing the angels that sinned, but, by throwing them into Tartarus, delivered them to pits of dense darkness to be reserved for judgment." This does not describe a place of fiery torment for human souls. It refers to the abased condition of demons who sinned and are now held in spiritual darkness awaiting final judgment.

Tartarus, therefore, must not be confused either with Sheol/Hades or with Gehenna. It is not the common grave. It is not the final destruction of the wicked. It is the restrained and degraded state of the demons under divine sentence. If one merges all these terms under a single popular idea of hell, the result is doctrinal chaos. But Scripture itself keeps them distinct. The grave is one thing. Final destruction is another. The restrained condition of evil spirits is another. Sound doctrine requires preserving those distinctions.

The Rich Man and Lazarus

One of the most frequently cited passages in defense of hellfire is Jesus' account of the rich man and Lazarus in Luke 16:19-31. But this passage must be read in harmony with Jesus' repeated use of parables and with the broader scriptural teaching that the dead are unconscious. Jesus often taught by illustration. Matthew 13:34 states plainly that He spoke many things to the crowds by illustrations. The account of the rich man and Lazarus is one such illustrative teaching, not a literal map of the afterlife.

The details themselves show this. If taken as a literal account, it would present the righteous and wicked conversing across a visible gulf, comfort and flame existing within speaking distance, and a drop of water on a fingertip offering relief from vast torment. But Jesus' point was not to give a topographical description of the state of the dead. His purpose was moral and prophetic. He was exposing the reversal awaiting the self-indulgent, unresponsive Jewish religious elite and the vindication of those whom they despised, while also showing that those who reject Moses and the Prophets will not be persuaded even if someone rises from the dead.

This reading is required not only by the parabolic form, but also by harmony with the rest of Scripture. The dead know nothing. Their thoughts perish. Jesus described death as sleep. Lazarus himself, in John 11, after being raised from death, gave no report of conscious bliss or torment because he had been asleep in death. Therefore Luke 16 cannot be used to overturn the consistent teaching of the rest of Scripture. It must be understood figuratively, in accordance with Jesus' use of parables and His practice of teaching spiritual truths through vivid imagery.

Hell Is Not Separation From God in Conscious Death

Some modern teachers, unwilling to defend literal flames, redefine hell as eternal conscious separation from God. But this view also conflicts with Scripture's teaching on the condition of the dead. The dead are not aware of separation from God because they are not conscious at all. Psalm 146:4 says their thoughts perish. Ecclesiastes says the dead know nothing. Death is the cessation of experience until resurrection. Therefore hell cannot be defined biblically as conscious awareness of alienation after death.

This does not mean the wicked avoid judgment. It means judgment is not to be redefined in ways Scripture itself does not use. The Bible's language for the final state of the wicked is destruction, perishing, being cut off, second death, and annihilation. These words all point away from endless conscious existence and toward the complete removal of the wicked from God's creation. The final punishment is everlasting in effect because it is irreversible, but it is still destruction and death, not another mode of eternal life.

The Moral Problem of Eternal Torment

Scripture not only fails to teach eternal torment; it also reveals the character of God in ways that stand against such an idea. "God is love" (1 John 4:8). He takes no delight in the death of the wicked, but desires that the wicked turn back from his way and keep living (Ezek. 33:11). He judged Israel for adopting practices that included burning sons and daughters in fire, saying such a thing "had not come up into my heart" (Jer. 7:31; 32:35). These revelations of God's character matter greatly.

The doctrine of endless conscious torment portrays God as preserving human beings forever in agony without hope, without purpose of restoration, and without end. Such a doctrine goes beyond the language of Scripture and conflicts with the Bible's own revelation of God's justice and love. Divine judgment is real, severe, and final. But final destruction is not the same as perpetual torture. Scripture teaches the former and not the latter.

This also affects the motivation for worship. God seeks those who worship Him in spirit and truth. He commands love for Him with the whole heart, soul, and mind (Matt. 22:37). The biblical motive for serving God is love, gratitude, reverence, and faith. Fear of endless torture may terrify, but it does not reflect the biblical basis of covenant relationship with Jehovah. The gospel calls sinners to repentance and faith because God has provided redemption in Christ, not because He threatens an endless inferno for all who do not comply.

Jesus, the Grave, and Resurrection

That Jesus Himself entered Hades when He died is one of the strongest biblical proofs against the common doctrine of hell. Acts 2:31 says His soul was not left in Hades. If Hades meant eternal torment, the statement would be impossible. But if Hades means the grave, the text makes perfect sense. Jesus died, entered the grave, and was raised on the third day. He was not abandoned there. Thus the biblical doctrine of hell in the sense of Sheol/Hades is inseparable from the doctrine of resurrection.

This is also why the resurrection narratives are so important. Scripture records several resurrections before Jesus and through His apostles: the widow's son in the days of Elijah, the Shunammite's son through Elisha, Jairus' daughter, the widow's son at Nain, Lazarus, Tabitha, Eutychus, and others. None of these resurrected persons returned with descriptions of conscious existence in torment or bliss. The silence is striking and entirely consistent with the doctrine that they had been asleep in death. Their restoration was restoration of life, not return from a fully conscious underworld or heavenly sphere.

The Final Destruction of Hell Itself

One of the most powerful biblical statements about hell comes in Revelation 20:13-14: "Death and Hades gave up the dead in them, and they were judged individually according to their deeds. And death and Hades were hurled into the lake of fire. This means the second death, the lake of fire." This text shows several essential truths at once.

First, Hades contains the dead. It is not itself the final state of punishment. It gives up the dead through resurrection. Second, Hades is temporary. It is later destroyed. Third, the lake of fire is explicitly defined as "the second death." Therefore the final punishment of the wicked is not best understood as endless conscious life in fire, but as second death, final and irreversible destruction under divine judgment.

The same pattern appears in Revelation 21:8, where the fearful, faithless, detestable, murderers, sexually immoral, spiritists, idolaters, and all liars have their part in the lake that burns with fire and sulfur, "which means the second death." Scripture itself defines the symbol. The lake of fire is second death. The wicked do not enter another immortal mode of existence. They enter final death under God's unchangeable sentence.

This reading also preserves the great promise of Revelation 21:4 that "death will be no more." If millions of the wicked remained eternally alive in torment, death would still in some sense endure as an everlasting condition of ruin. But Scripture says death itself is abolished. The last enemy is destroyed. Evil is removed, not preserved forever in a conscious counter-realm. The universe is cleansed, not eternally divided between joy and endless torment.

The Biblical Hope Against Hell

The biblical doctrine of hell is severe, but it is also coherent and hope-filled. It does not flatter sin. The wicked face real judgment. The grave holds the dead. The final end of the unrepentantly wicked is destruction. Gehenna signifies irreversible ruin. The second death excludes all hope of future life. These truths should sober every reader of Scripture. God is not mocked. Men will reap what they sow.

Yet the Bible's message is not dominated by terror but by redemption. God has provided a ransom in Jesus Christ. Christ died, entered the grave, and rose again. By His resurrection He broke the power of death and guarantees future resurrection for those in the memorial tombs. Those who respond in faith and remain loyal to God through Christ receive the hope of everlasting life, whether in the heavenly calling for those appointed to reign with Christ or in everlasting life on the restored earth under His kingdom administration. The gospel does not offer mere survival of an immortal soul. It offers life from God as gift through Christ.

Explaining Hell According to Scripture

When the whole biblical witness is allowed to stand, the doctrine becomes clear. Sheol and Hades mean the grave, the common realm of the dead. Those there are unconscious. Gehenna signifies final destruction, not eternal torment. Tartarus describes the abased condition of sinning angels, not the afterlife of men. The dead do not think, plan, suffer, or praise. Death is the wage of sin. The soul dies. The only hope beyond death is resurrection by the power of God. Final judgment ends in everlasting life for the righteous and second death for the wicked. The grave itself is emptied and destroyed, and death will be no more.

This doctrine is in harmony with creation, with the sentence upon Adam, with the Psalms, with the Prophets, with Jesus' teaching, with the apostolic letters, and with Revelation. It is also in harmony with the character of Jehovah, who is just, holy, and loving. The wicked are not preserved forever for torture. They are finally destroyed. The righteous are not naturally immortal. They receive life as God's gift. And the universe will not forever echo with the screams of the damned. It will be cleansed of death, sorrow, pain, and rebellion, because Jehovah through His Christ will bring all enemies to nothing.

Therefore hell must be explained biblically, not traditionally. The grave is real. Judgment is real. Final destruction is real. But eternal conscious torment is not the doctrine of Scripture. The dead are asleep in the grave until resurrection. The wicked who persist in rebellion face irreversible destruction in the second death. And the faithful may look beyond death and the grave to the resurrection hope and the everlasting life that God has promised through Jesus Christ. Only this understanding preserves the full force of the biblical language about death, judgment, and the triumph of God's kingdom.

CHAPTER 11 Explaining the Resurrection Hope: The Righteous, the Unrighteous, and the Wicked

The Centrality of the Resurrection Hope

The resurrection hope stands at the heart of biblical eschatology. It is not an incidental doctrine, nor is it merely one comforting theme among many. Scripture presents resurrection as the divine answer to death, the public vindication of God's justice, the proof of Christ's authority, and the means by which Jehovah brings human history to its appointed judgment and restoration. The biblical hope is therefore not founded on the alleged immortality of the soul. It is founded on the power of God to raise the dead. Without resurrection, death would remain master over mankind, the grave would retain its captives, and the promises of everlasting life would have no historical fulfillment. But because Christ has been raised, the dead are not beyond the reach of Jehovah's purpose, and the future of mankind is not locked in the silence of the grave.

This is why the New Testament repeatedly places resurrection at the center of the Christian proclamation. Paul tells the Corinthians that if Christ has not been raised, their faith is vain and those who have fallen asleep in Christ have perished (1 Cor. 15:14-18). His argument assumes the full reality of death and the absolute necessity of resurrection. Christ's resurrection is not merely a sign of survival after death. It is the firstfruits of those asleep in death, the beginning of a divinely ordered sequence by which death itself will be brought to nothing (1 Cor. 15:20-26). In the same way, Jesus identifies Himself as "the resurrection and the life" and tells Martha that the one exercising faith in Him will come to life even though he dies (John 11:25). He does not direct hope toward a naturally immortal element within man. He directs hope toward Himself as the One through whom Jehovah restores life.

The resurrection hope also governs the meaning of Judgment Day. If the dead are truly dead, unconscious in the grave, then judgment must include God's act of calling the dead forth into life again. That is exactly what Scripture teaches. Daniel speaks of those sleeping in the dust awakening. Jesus says all those in the memorial tombs will hear His voice and come out. Paul affirms a resurrection of both the righteous and the unrighteous. Revelation speaks of the first resurrection and of the broader dealings with the dead in the thousand-year and post-thousand-year framework. The grave is real, but it is not final. Death is an enemy, but it is not invincible. Christ's kingdom includes resurrection because God's purpose in Christ extends beyond the grave.

The Old Testament Foundation in Daniel

The clearest Old Testament text for the resurrection hope is Daniel 12:2: "And many of those asleep in the dust of the ground will awake, these to everlasting life, and those to reproaches—to everlasting abhorrence." This passage is remarkable for both its clarity and its seriousness. Daniel does not speak of disembodied survival. He speaks of those asleep in the dust of the ground. The image is exact. The dead are not portrayed as consciously active in heaven or in torment. They are asleep in the dust. Yet they do not remain there forever. They awake by divine action.

The text also establishes that resurrection and final outcome are related but not identical. Daniel speaks of awakening, and then of two everlasting outcomes. Some awake to everlasting life. Others awake to reproaches and everlasting abhorrence. This means resurrection itself is not the final blessing in every case. Resurrection brings the dead into God's judicial purpose. The final result depends on the category in which they stand before God. Daniel therefore already lays the groundwork for distinguishing between resurrection, judgment, and everlasting outcome.

At the same time, Daniel's wording must be handled with precision. The two final outcomes in the verse are everlasting in result. Everlasting life is one. Everlasting abhorrence is the other. But the wider biblical witness shows that those brought under God's judicial administration are not all to be treated as one undifferentiated class. Daniel presents the final polarity of everlasting outcomes. Later revelation provides more precision regarding the categories of persons brought into resurrection and judgment. This is why a historical-grammatical reading must be canonical as well as immediate. Daniel provides the prophetic foundation; Jesus, Paul, and Revelation bring fuller definition.

Daniel 12 also places resurrection in the setting of the time of the end, the unparalleled distress, and Michael's decisive intervention on behalf of God's people. Resurrection is therefore not a detached philosophical doctrine. It belongs to the final movement of God's kingdom purpose. The same God who governs the rise and fall of empires, who limits beastly dominion, and who delivers His people at the appointed time also raises the dead. The kingdom of God is not merely about surviving history. It is about God overturning death itself.

Jesus and the Resurrection of Life and Judgment

Jesus gives the most direct statement of general resurrection in John 5:28-29: "Do not be amazed at this, because the hour is coming in which all those in the memorial tombs will hear His voice and come out, those who did good things to a resurrection of life, those who practiced vile things to a resurrection of judgment." This statement is profoundly important because it shows both the scope and the distinction within resurrection. Jesus says that "all those in the memorial tombs" will hear His voice. That means the resurrection authority entrusted to the Son is comprehensive in reach. The grave does not retain anyone independently of His command. Yet the outcomes are not identical. Some come out to a resurrection of life. Others come out to a resurrection of judgment.

The expression "resurrection of life" is clear enough in its general force. It denotes resurrection issuing in life under divine approval. The expression "resurrection of judgment," however, has often been misunderstood. It does not require that all who experience it are raised only to be immediately condemned without any ordered process under God's kingdom administration. The Greek term for judgment can denote judicial assessment, evaluation, decision, and the process by which a case is brought under righteous determination. In the light of the broader biblical framework, this means that resurrection can bring a person into the sphere of Jehovah's judicial administration under Christ, where the final outcome is not detached from response to the conditions and truth made known under that administration.

This point is especially important when John 5 is read alongside Acts 24:15 and Daniel 12:2. Jesus states the two great result-categories in terms of life and judgment. Daniel states the two everlasting outcomes in terms of everlasting life and everlasting abhorrence. But Paul in Acts 24:15 gives an intermediate distinction of enormous value when he says there is to be "a resurrection both of the righteous and the unrighteous." This means that the class brought into resurrection and judgment is not exhausted by simply saying "saved" and "damned" in a crude sense. Scripture requires more care. The righteous are one class. The unrighteous are another. The finally wicked are yet another. A responsible doctrine of resurrection must preserve those distinctions.

Jesus' language in John 5 also reinforces the fact that resurrection is not the continuation of conscious life after death in another sphere. Those in the memorial tombs hear His voice and come out. That means they were in the tombs. The image is not one of souls descending from heaven or ascending from torment to rejoin bodies. It is the Son of God summoning the dead from the grave. His voice reaches into death because the Father has granted Him to have life in Himself and has given Him authority to execute judgment (John 5:26-27). Resurrection and judgment are therefore inseparable from the authority of Christ. He is both Life-Giver and Judge.

Paul and the Resurrection of the Righteous and the Unrighteous

Acts 24:15 is one of the most decisive texts in the whole subject: "I have hope toward God, which hope these men also themselves entertain, that there is going to be a resurrection of both the righteous and the unrighteous." Paul does not speak here of a resurrection of the righteous only. Nor does he speak of one undifferentiated resurrection in which no moral distinctions exist. He clearly names two classes: the righteous and the unrighteous. This requires precision in interpretation.

The righteous are those approved by Jehovah. They are those who lived in covenant loyalty according to the light and responsibility given them. Their resurrection belongs to the category Jesus calls a resurrection of life and Daniel calls awakening to everlasting life. For such persons, resurrection is vindication and confirmed life under God's favor. Their approval does not arise from natural moral superiority, but from Jehovah's gracious acceptance of those who live in faith and obedience according to His revealed will.

The unrighteous are different. They are not described as righteous servants of Jehovah, yet Paul still includes them in the resurrection hope. This means they are not to be collapsed automatically into the finally wicked. They are those who did not live as righteous servants under the full light or full obedience required, yet who are not presented as settled, culpable, irredeemable rebels already beyond all possible judicial consideration under Christ's kingdom. Their resurrection is therefore associated with judgment in the sense of evaluation under Jehovah's appointed administration. It is not a resurrection to automatic approval, but neither should it be carelessly defined as immediate irreversible condemnation without any distinction from the wicked.

This is why canonical synthesis is essential. If Acts 24:15 speaks of the righteous and the unrighteous, then any doctrine of resurrection that merges the unrighteous directly into the final wickedness of irrevocable destruction fails to preserve Paul's distinction. At the same time, no doctrine may imply that unrighteousness is harmless or that resurrection guarantees life regardless of response. The unrighteous are raised into judgment, and judgment is real. But judgment, as Scripture uses the term, can include accountable assessment under God's kingdom administration, not merely instant re-condemnation for a past life already ended in death.

Distinguishing the Righteous, the Unrighteous, and the Wicked

A sound doctrine of resurrection requires three moral categories to remain distinct: the righteous, the unrighteous, and the wicked. If these are blended together, confusion follows immediately. Daniel 12:2 and John 5:28-29 establish the reality of two everlasting outcomes. Acts 24:15 clarifies that among those brought into resurrection there are the righteous and the unrighteous. The finally wicked, however, are a distinct class associated with irreversible destruction rather than restorative resurrection.

The righteous are those approved by Jehovah. They are raised to life. In one sense, all righteous resurrection is resurrection to life because it issues in divine approval and the gift of life under God's kingdom. Yet even within the righteous there are distinctions of role. Revelation 20:4-6 speaks of the blessed and holy company who share in the first resurrection. They reign with Christ for the thousand years, serve as priests of God and of the Christ, and over them the second death has no authority. This is a distinct resurrection company, not a flat description of all the righteous without differentiation. These are the royal-priestly rulers associated with Christ's heavenly administration.

The unrighteous are raised into judgment. This class consists of those not counted among the righteous servants of Jehovah in their former life, yet not portrayed as finally and irrevocably wicked beyond all judicial consideration. Their resurrection brings them into the sphere of Christ's righteous rule, where divine standards are applied and response matters. The language of judgment therefore should be handled carefully. It does not require that the unrighteous are raised merely to hear a sentence already fixed in exactly the same way as the final wicked. Rather, they are raised into Jehovah's judicial order, where their outcome is determined in connection with divine truth, righteous administration, and accountable response.

The wicked, by contrast, are those whose rebellion is settled, culpable, and final. Scripture describes their end in terms of destruction, second death, Gehenna, and annihilation rather than restorative resurrection hope. Their outcome corresponds to Daniel's language of everlasting abhorrence and to Revelation's second death. They are not portrayed as a class returning to life in order to be rehabilitated under the kingdom. Their end is irreversible removal. This distinction preserves the moral force of Scripture. God is just. He does not confuse the unrighteous with the righteous, nor does He confuse the unrighteous with the finally wicked. Each category must be allowed to stand where the text places it.

The First Resurrection

Revelation 20:4-6 introduces a crucial distinction within the doctrine of resurrection: "And I saw thrones, and those who sat down on them were given authority to judge... And they came to life and ruled as kings with the Christ for the thousand years. This is the first resurrection. Happy and holy is anyone having part in the first resurrection; over these the second death has no authority, but they will be priests of God and of the Christ, and they will rule as kings with him for the thousand years." This passage must be respected in its order and force.

The first resurrection belongs to the blessed and holy reigning company. It is tied to priestly and kingly administration with Christ. This group is distinct from "the rest of the dead," whom John immediately contrasts with them in Revelation 20:5. Therefore, the first resurrection is not a vague synonym for every resurrection whatever. It is a specific resurrection of the royal-priestly company who share in Christ's heavenly reign.

This fits the wider biblical pattern already seen. Paul's teaching on transformation in 1 Corinthians 15 and the gathering to Christ in 1 Thessalonians 4 belongs specifically to those inheriting the heavenly kingdom in that ruling sense. Flesh and blood cannot inherit that kingdom in its heavenly form, so transformation and incorruption are necessary. Revelation 20 shows the result of that calling. Those who share in the first resurrection reign with Christ. The second death has no authority over them because their standing is confirmed and their role in the kingdom administration is established.

This resurrection must also be placed before the thousand years, since the text itself does so. Christ returns in judgment in Revelation 19, the beast and false prophet are destroyed, Satan is bound, and then this reigning company is described as coming to life and ruling with Christ during the thousand years. The first resurrection, therefore, belongs to the opening of the millennial kingdom era.

The Rest of the Dead

Revelation 20:5 adds, "The rest of the dead did not come to life until the thousand years were ended." This is one of the more difficult statements in the chapter, but it must not be ignored or forced into a simplistic shape. At minimum, it establishes a distinction between the first-resurrection company and all others. John is not allowing readers to merge the blessed and holy reigning class with every other dead person. The first resurrection is set apart. The rest of the dead stand in a different relation to the thousand-year framework.

At the same time, the wider biblical witness remains clear that there is a resurrection of the righteous and the unrighteous and that all in the memorial tombs hear Christ's voice. Therefore, Revelation 20:5 must not be used to cancel Acts 24:15 or John 5:28-29. Rather, it preserves the special distinction of the first-resurrection company while leaving the broader dealings with the dead to be understood within the total kingdom framework described by Scripture. The point is not to erase the resurrection of the righteous and the unrighteous, but to emphasize that the reigning company's resurrection is unique in role, timing, and status.

This also helps guard against a flat reading of resurrection. Scripture does not present one undifferentiated mass-event in which all categories, outcomes, and functions are collapsed together. There is order. Christ is the firstfruits. Then those who belong to Him in the specific order God has appointed. The first resurrection belongs to the kingly-priestly company. The broader resurrection and judgment process stands in relation to the thousand-year kingdom administration and the final phases of divine judgment.

Resurrection and Judgment Are Related but Not Identical

One of the most important hermeneutical points in the entire doctrine is that resurrection and judgment are related but not identical. Resurrection is the act of being brought back to life by God. Judgment is the divine judicial determination of one's standing and outcome under His righteous standards. Sometimes the two are so closely connected that they are spoken of almost together, as in John 5:28-29. But they should not be carelessly collapsed.

This matters especially for the unrighteous. If resurrection and final condemnation are made absolutely identical in every case, then Acts 24:15 loses its force. But if judgment is allowed its biblical range, including assessment and accountable decision under Christ's administration, then the unrighteous can be understood as raised into divine judicial process rather than automatically merged into the finally wicked. This does not weaken judgment. It clarifies it. Jehovah's judgment is not confused or careless. He judges according to truth, light, accountability, and response.

For the righteous, resurrection and life belong together because their standing before God is favorable. For the royal-priestly company of the first resurrection, that standing includes reign with Christ and immunity from the second death. For the unrighteous, resurrection brings them under divine rule where judgment determines their final outcome. For the wicked, final judgment ends in destruction, not restorative life. The distinctions must remain in place if the text is to be honored.

Everlasting Life and Immortality

Another important distinction is between everlasting life and immortality. These are not always interchangeable terms in Scripture. Everlasting life refers to life of endless duration granted by God. Immortality, in the stricter New Testament sense, refers to deathlessness or incorruptibility bestowed in a specific way. First Corinthians 15:53-54 speaks of "this mortal" putting on immortality and "this which is corruptible" putting on incorruption. First Timothy 6:16 says God alone has immortality inherently. Therefore immortality is not a natural possession of man and is not to be assumed in every use of everlasting life language.

This distinction is useful because Scripture presents the heavenly rulers in a unique relation to incorruption and immortality. Their transformation is explicit. At the same time, the broader promise of everlasting life for the righteous under God's kingdom does not require us to collapse every usage into exactly the same technical category. God grants life as He wills according to His purpose. The key point is that everlasting life is a gift, not a natural possession, and resurrection is the means by which God restores and confirms that life.

The Resurrection Hope for the Righteous

The hope of the righteous is sure. Jesus says those who did good things come out to a resurrection of life. Daniel says some awake to everlasting life. Paul says there is a resurrection of the righteous. Revelation says the blessed and holy share in the first resurrection and reign with Christ. The righteous are therefore not forgotten in death. Their names are not lost to God. The grave does not erase Jehovah's memory of them.

This hope also extends beyond merely being alive again. Resurrection is restoration under God's favor and within His kingdom purpose. For some, this means participation in the heavenly ruling body with Christ. For the broader body of the righteous, it means life under the kingdom administration in the restored order God establishes. The Bible does not treat resurrection as a bare return to earthly existence with no further redemptive meaning. It is part of the triumph of Christ over death and part of the unfolding of Jehovah's purpose to fill the earth with righteousness.

This is why faithfulness in the present matters so deeply. The righteous are not righteous by natural merit. They are those who live in faith, obedience, and loyalty according to the light God has given. Resurrection to life is therefore not an abstract reward disconnected from the moral shape of one's life. It is God's public affirmation of those who belonged to Him.

The Resurrection and Judgment of the Unrighteous

Acts 24:15 makes it impossible to exclude the unrighteous from the resurrection hope altogether. There is to be a resurrection both of the righteous and of the unrighteous. This is not a loose statement or a careless phrase. Paul's wording must be allowed its force. The unrighteous are a real class distinct from the righteous. Yet the fact that they are included in resurrection shows that Jehovah's judicial administration is broader and more ordered than a simplistic scheme would allow.

The unrighteous are not those already confirmed in everlasting life. Neither are they automatically to be equated with the finally wicked whose end is destruction. They are raised into judgment, that is, into the sphere of Christ's righteous administration and decision. This means they are brought under the kingdom in a way that renders response, accountability, and divine verdict meaningful. Their resurrection itself is already a testimony that God's purpose in Christ extends beyond the grave and that death is not the last word over them.

This does not mean the unrighteous are guaranteed life regardless of their condition. The kingdom of Christ is not morally indifferent. Judgment is real. But the text requires that they be treated as a distinct class under divine evaluation. That is why the category is important. If all unrighteous persons are simply called wicked in the final sense, Paul's distinction loses its value. Scripture instead permits a more careful doctrine: the unrighteous are raised into judgment under

Christ's administration, and their final outcome depends on divine judicial determination in that context.

The Final State of the Wicked

Scripture's teaching concerning the wicked is severe and final. Psalm 145:20 says Jehovah will annihilate all the wicked. Jesus warns of Gehenna as the place of destruction of both body and soul. Paul speaks of destruction for those not obeying the good news. Revelation calls the final end "the second death." Daniel 12:2 speaks of awakening to reproaches and everlasting abhorrence. These expressions must not be softened into universal hope, nor should they be transformed into eternal conscious torment. They point to irreversible destruction and final rejection.

The wicked are therefore a distinct category. They are not to be confused with the righteous, obviously, but neither are they simply interchangeable with the unrighteous in Acts 24:15. The wicked are those finally judged as culpable, settled rebels against Jehovah. Their outcome is not restorative resurrection leading toward life, but permanent removal under divine judgment. The second death has no reversal. Gehenna signifies final destruction. Everlasting abhorrence describes the enduring contempt attached to that final divine rejection.

This preserves both justice and clarity. Jehovah does not perpetually preserve the wicked in conscious suffering. Neither does He treat wickedness as inconsequential. He removes it completely. The final universe is cleansed of rebellion, not endlessly haunted by it.

Resurrection in Relation to the Millennium

The thousand-year reign of Christ provides the kingdom framework within which the resurrection hope reaches ordered expression. Revelation 20 does not present resurrection and judgment as a single instant without sequence. It presents the first resurrection of the reigning company, then the thousand-year rule, then the later dealing with the rest of the dead in relation to the great white throne and the final defeat of death and Hades. This means the resurrection doctrine must be integrated into the millennial administration of Christ rather than detached from it.

That framework is hopeful. Christ's kingdom is not a bare judicial tribunal without redemptive purpose. It is the administration by which He brings all enemies under His feet, including death itself. First Corinthians 15 says He must reign until He has put all enemies under His feet, and the last enemy is death (1 Cor. 15:25-26). That reign includes resurrection, judgment, and the final abolition of death. The kingdom is therefore the arena in which the resurrection hope comes to completion.

This also shows why resurrection is not merely an appendix to the gospel. It belongs to the very reign of Christ. If He is King, He must conquer death. If He is Judge, He must summon the dead. If He is Life-Giver, He must raise those in the tombs. The millennium is thus not a doctrinal distraction from resurrection, but one of the great contexts in which resurrection and judgment are worked out under His administration.

The Great White Throne and Final Outcome

Revelation 20:11-15 presents the great white throne. The dead, great and small, stand before the throne, scrolls are opened, another scroll is opened which is the scroll of life, and the dead are judged according to their deeds as these stand written in the scrolls. Then death and Hades are hurled into the lake of fire, which means the second death. This scene is solemn and final. It shows that resurrection and judgment move toward a complete and decisive conclusion.

The great white throne also confirms that resurrection does not erase accountability. Those raised stand before God's judicial process. Their deeds matter. Divine memory is exact. Yet the scene ends not in endless ambiguity but in finality. Those not found written in the scroll of life are hurled into the lake of fire, the second death. This means the final state of the wicked is destruction, not perpetual life in another form. At the same time, the fact that death and Hades are themselves destroyed shows that the resurrection hope has reached its triumph.

The grave is emptied. Death no longer rules. God's judgment is complete.

The Hope That Death Does Not Have the Final Word

The resurrection doctrine is hopeful because it means death does not have the final word. The grave is real, but it is not sovereign. Men die, but they do not pass beyond the reach of Jehovah's memory. Christ has the keys of death and of Hades (Rev. 1:18). He is the appointed Judge and Life-Giver. Those asleep in the dust will awake. Those in the memorial tombs will hear His voice. The righteous are not forgotten. Even the unrighteous are not beyond the ordered judicial reach of God's kingdom. The finally wicked, however, will not corrupt the new creation forever, for their end is destruction.

This hope is profoundly different from the philosophical notion of the immortal soul. It is better because it is biblical. It preserves the seriousness of death, the necessity of Christ's resurrection, the centrality of divine judgment, and the gift-character of eternal life. It also preserves the moral distinctions Scripture itself insists on. Not all men stand before God in the same way. The righteous, the unrighteous, and the wicked must not be confused.

The Full Doctrine of the Resurrection Hope

When all the relevant passages are held together, the doctrine may be stated clearly. Daniel 12:2 establishes resurrection from the dust and two everlasting outcomes. Jesus in John 5 teaches that all in the memorial tombs hear His voice and come out, some to life and some to judgment. Paul in Acts 24 affirms a resurrection of both the righteous and the unrighteous, requiring distinction between those categories. Revelation 20 identifies a first resurrection for the blessed and holy reigning company, then places the broader dealings with the dead within the thousand-year and post-thousand-year framework, culminating in the great white throne and the destruction of death itself.

The righteous are raised to everlasting life, and the first-resurrection company reigns with Christ as priests and kings. The unrighteous are raised into judgment, that is, into Jehovah's judicial administration under Christ's kingdom, where divine evaluation and accountable response determine outcome. The wicked are not a merely synonymous term for the unrighteous. They are the finally condemned rebels whose end is second death, everlasting abhorrence, and irreversible destruction.

This doctrine preserves the full seriousness and the full hopefulness of Judgment Day. The grave does not defeat Jehovah's purpose. The dead are not beyond Christ's voice. Death is an enemy, but not an unconquerable one. Resurrection is real, judgment is real, everlasting life is real, and final destruction is real. The kingdom of God, therefore, is not only about surviving the end of the present age. It is about Jehovah through Christ summoning the dead, judging in righteousness, rewarding the faithful, dealing justly with the unrighteous, and finally removing wickedness forever. That is the resurrection hope in its full biblical framework, and it stands among the most glorious assurances in all of Scripture because it declares that through Jesus Christ the grave will not have the final word.

CHAPTER 12 Explaining the Millennium, the Final Rebellion, and the Great White Throne

The Millennium in the Flow of Biblical Prophecy

The millennium is not an isolated doctrine suspended above the rest of prophecy. It stands within a definite sequence revealed in Scripture. Christ returns in judgment, the beast and false prophet are overthrown, Satan is bound, the first-resurrection company reigns with Christ for a thousand years, Satan is later released for a short time, the final rebellion is crushed, and then comes the great white throne with the final abolition of death and Hades. This order is neither accidental nor decorative. It is the Spirit-given structure of Revelation 19–20, and it must be respected if the doctrine of last things is to remain governed by the text rather than by later systems.

Much confusion has entered the discussion because some have treated the thousand years as though they were only a vague symbol for the present church age. But the immediate context resists that reading. Revelation 19 presents the visible appearing of Christ in judgment against the beastly order. Revelation 20 then moves forward, not backward, to show what follows that victory. The dragon is bound so that he might not deceive the nations any longer until the thousand years were ended. The faithful reigning company comes to life and reigns with Christ for a thousand years. Only after the thousand years does Satan's final release occur. Only after that release and the destruction of the final rebellion does John see the great white throne. The sequence is plain. The millennium is a distinct kingdom era following Christ's victory over the present anti-God order and preceding the final post-millennial rebellion and the last judicial phase.

This premillennial order is also in harmony with the broader prophetic pattern. Daniel 2 shows the kingdom of God striking and replacing the succession of human empires. Daniel 7 shows beastly dominion judged, the Son of Man receiving dominion, and the holy ones sharing in kingdom rule. First Corinthians 15 says Christ must reign until He has put all enemies under His feet, and the last enemy to be abolished is death. Revelation 20 provides the great kingdom stage in which that reign advances toward its final victory over every hostile power. The millennium, then, is not a speculative curiosity. It is the revealed era of Christ's kingdom administration between the overthrow of the beastly order and the last abolition of death.

Satan Bound for a Thousand Years

Revelation 20:1-3 begins the chapter with one of the most decisive transitions in the Apocalypse: "And I saw an angel coming down out of heaven with the key of the abyss and a great chain in his hand. And he seized the dragon, the original serpent, who is the Devil and Satan, and bound him for a thousand years, and threw him into the abyss and shut it and sealed it over him, so that he might not deceive the nations any longer until the thousand years were ended. After these things he must be released for a short time." The passage is rich in imagery, yet the meaning is not obscure. The one who has deceived the inhabited earth, energized the beastly order, and gathered the kings for war is now decisively restrained by divine authority.

The key of the abyss and the great chain are not best understood as literal hardware for a material prison. Revelation constantly uses objects to signify real authority over spiritual realities. The point is not that heaven requires iron links to subdue a spirit creature. The point is that Satan is fully subject to Jehovah's decree. The abyss is the divinely appointed place or condition of imprisonment in which satanic activity is restrained and sealed off from free operation among the nations. The language of being thrown in, shut in, and sealed over accumulates to emphasize the completeness of the restraint. Satan is not merely weakened. He is confined.

The purpose clause interprets the binding: "so that he might not deceive the nations any longer until the thousand years were ended." This is the heart of the passage. Satan's distinguishing work in Revelation is deception. He deceives the whole inhabited earth, the kings, and the nations. During the millennium that deceiving work is suspended. The nations are no longer under the same dragon-energized deception that characterized the beastly age. This alone shows that the thousand years cannot be merely another description of the present age. The present world is plainly still under deception, false worship, and rebellion. Revelation 20 describes a condition radically different from that.

The text also says Satan "must be released for a short time" after the thousand years. The word "must" matters. His release is not an escape. It is not a failure in divine government. It is part of God's decree. The entire millennium, from binding to release, is governed from heaven. The dragon is not sovereign in his activity, and he is not sovereign in his restraint. He moves only within what God permits. This means that even the final outbreak of rebellion serves the purpose of God and not the triumph of evil.

The Thousand Years as a Real Kingdom Era

The repeated expression "a thousand years" should be allowed its ordinary force within the context. Nothing in the immediate passage suggests that John means an undefined or timeless symbol for the whole church age. On the contrary, he presents the thousand years as a bounded period following the overthrow of the beast and preceding Satan's short release. The duration is repeated so that the reader cannot miss its importance. To empty it of temporal significance is to flatten the chapter's structure and blur the distinction between Christ's present heavenly rule and this distinct future kingdom phase.

This does not mean that the number is bare arithmetic detached from theological significance. The thousand years is certainly a God-appointed, complete, measured era of kingdom administration. Yet theological significance does not cancel temporal force. Scripture often uses numbers that are both meaningful and real within the vision. Here the thousand years marks the duration of Satan's restraint, the reign of the first-resurrection company with Christ, and the period after which the final rebellion occurs. The chapter's sequence requires a real period, not a vague symbol floating across the whole age.

This kingdom era must also be read positively. The millennium is not merely the absence of Satanic deception. It is the active reign of Christ and His royal-priestly company. The earth is not left in suspension between the destruction of the beast and the final judgment. Rather, the reign of Christ moves forward under conditions fundamentally different from the present age. Satan is restrained. The kingdom administration is in place. The first-resurrection company shares in priestly and kingly service. The thousand years is therefore a defined stage in the outworking of God's purpose, not an empty interval.

The First Resurrection and the Reigning Company

Revelation 20:4-6 describes the positive heart of the millennium: "And I saw thrones, and they sat on them, and judgment was given to them. And I saw the souls of those who had been beheaded because of the testimony of Jesus and because of the word of God, and those who had not worshiped the beast or his image and had not received the mark on their forehead and on their hand; and they came to life and reigned with Christ for a thousand years. (The rest of the dead did not come to life until the thousand years were completed.) This is the first resurrection. Happy and holy is the one having part in the first resurrection; over these the second death has no authority, but they will be priests of God and of Christ and will reign with Him for the thousand years."

The first thing John sees is thrones. That means authority, kingdom order, and delegated rule. This is not mere honor in heaven detached from the administration of God's purpose. "Judgment was given to them" recalls Daniel 7, where thrones are set and judgment is rendered in favor of the holy ones of the Most High. John's point is that the thousand-year period is a kingdom era of real judicial and governing significance under Christ.

The company he then sees is described as those who suffered for their testimony to Jesus and the word of God, those who refused the beast and would not receive his mark. These are the faithful conquerors of the final anti-God order. "Souls" here does not imply the natural immortality of man. It identifies the very persons whom the beastly world put to death and whom God now brings into public vindication. The emphasis is that those who were condemned by the world are acknowledged by heaven.

John then says, "they came to life." In the immediate context, after Christ's return in judgment and before the thousand-year reign, the most natural meaning is resurrection. This is not merely survival of influence or continuation of memory. It is coming to life from death. John himself immediately names it: "This is the first resurrection." Therefore the reigning company is a resurrected company. They are not merely honored martyrs in an abstract sense. They are the blessed and holy participants in the first resurrection.

The first resurrection is first not merely in abstract numbering but in privileged relation to the kingdom. It precedes the later dealings with "the rest of the dead" and belongs to the opening of the millennial reign. Over this company the second death has no authority. That means their standing before God is secure and beyond final condemnation. They are priests of God and of Christ, which signifies consecrated nearness and service, and they reign with Him for the thousand years, which signifies participation in His kingdom administration.

This harmonizes with the broader biblical distinction between the select company called to heavenly rulership and the broader body of the righteous who receive everlasting life under that kingdom administration. Revelation had already presented a royal-priestly body made a kingdom and priests to God. Here that role is tied directly to the thousand years. The first resurrection, therefore, belongs to the heavenly ruling company and marks the beginning of the millennial kingdom era.

The Rest of the Dead and the Millennial Framework

Revelation 20:5 introduces a contrast: "The rest of the dead did not come to life until the thousand years were completed." This statement must be read in harmony with the broader biblical witness regarding the resurrection of the righteous and the unrighteous. John's immediate purpose is to distinguish the first-resurrection company from all others. The blessed and holy come to life and reign at the beginning of the thousand years. The rest of the dead do not come to life in that same privileged way at that same point.

This means the chapter preserves order and distinction. It does not flatten every resurrection and every outcome into one undifferentiated instant. The first resurrection belongs to the kingly-priestly company. The broader dealings with the dead stand in a different relation to the thousand-year framework. This is consistent with Acts 24:15, which speaks of a resurrection of both the righteous and the unrighteous, and with John 5:28-29, where all in the memorial tombs hear Christ's voice and come out, some to life and some to judgment. Revelation 20 adds kingdom order and sequence to that broader testimony.

The point is not that John contradicts those earlier passages, but that he provides further structural definition. The millennial reign is the kingdom setting in which resurrection, judgment, and final outcome are brought toward completion. Therefore one must not detach the resurrection hope from the thousand years, nor should one collapse the thousand years into a vague symbol that cannot sustain these distinctions.

The Priestly and Royal Character of the Millennium

The millennium is not merely a period of restored conditions. It is a kingdom administration. Those sharing in the first resurrection are called priests of God and of Christ and reign with Him. This language is vital because it shows that the thousand years involves both rule and sacred service. Priestly language points to consecration, mediation, and nearness to God. Royal language points to authority, judgment, and kingdom administration. Together they show that the millennium is the era in which Christ and His appointed co-rulers carry forward Jehovah's purpose in an ordered and public way.

This royal-priestly structure also fulfills earlier promises. Jesus told His faithful apostles they would sit on thrones in His kingdom. Revelation earlier spoke of a kingdom and priests. Daniel foresaw the holy ones receiving the kingdom. The millennium is where those strands visibly meet. The beastly order has been judged, Satan is restrained, and the holy ones who conquered now reign under Christ.

This does not mean the millennium is an end in itself. It is a kingdom phase moving history toward the final abolition of all enemies. Christ must reign until every enemy is under His feet. The millennium is thus administrative and progressive. It is the era in which the kingdom, under radically changed conditions of satanic restraint, advances God's judicial and restorative purpose toward the final removal of rebellion and death.

The Release of Satan After the Thousand Years

Revelation 20:7-8 states: "When the thousand years are completed, Satan will be released from his prison, and will come out to deceive the nations in the four corners of the earth, Gog and Magog, to gather them together for the war. The number of these is as the sand of the sea." This release is one of the most solemn and revealing moments in the chapter. It shows that the millennium does not end in quiet fading, but in one final exposure of evil after the thousand years have fully run their course.

The release occurs only "when the thousand years are completed." That means it is not an interruption of the reign, but a post-millennial event. Again the sequence must be respected. Satan is bound during the thousand years, released after them, and destroyed only after that final outbreak of rebellion. His release is permitted by God and serves the divine purpose of exposing rebellion one last time. The devil does not break free independently. He is released under decree.

The immediate thing he does upon release is exactly what his character demands: he deceives the nations. That confirms that deception is his defining work. During the thousand years that work was suspended. Once released, it resumes immediately. This shows the millennium really was an era distinct from the present age of deception. It also shows that evil never becomes self-justifying or creative under Satan's influence. It remains parasitic, deceptive, and hostile to God.

The nations are described as being in the four corners of the earth, which indicates breadth and global scope rather than a merely local disturbance. The names Gog and Magog, drawn from Ezekiel 38–39, function typologically to describe the final collective enemy of God's people. They are not to be reduced simplistically to one modern nation or ethnic bloc. Revelation is not giving a newspaper identity key. It is using Ezekiel's prophetic pattern to depict the last broad rebellion against the kingdom of God after the millennial period.

The Final Rebellion of Gog and Magog

Revelation 20:9 says, "And they advanced over the broad plain of the earth and encircled the camp of the holy ones and the beloved city. But fire came down out of heaven and devoured them." This verse is striking for both the scale of the rebellion and the swiftness of its end. The nations surround the camp of the holy ones and the beloved city, which signifies the covenant people of God in the sphere of His kingdom favor. Yet no prolonged battle follows. No uncertain struggle occurs. Fire comes down from heaven and devours them.

This makes clear that the final rebellion is not a serious threat to God's sovereignty. It is an exposure of what rebellion is when Satan is loosed and a final demonstration that evil, however numerous, cannot stand before heaven's judgment. Their number is like the sand of the sea, but their multitude gives them no advantage. Divine judgment ends the revolt immediately. The kingdom of God is never placed in jeopardy.

The "camp of the holy ones" and the "beloved city" should not be reduced to old-covenant ethnic restoration apart from Christ. In Revelation the covenant center belongs to God and the Lamb. The point is that the final hostility of the nations is directed against the people of God under His kingdom order. Yet that hostility succeeds only in exposing itself to destruction. The same pattern was already seen in Armageddon. The gathered rebels meet divine intervention and are removed. But here the setting is different. This is after the thousand years, after Satan's release, and before the great white throne. Therefore it must be distinguished from Armageddon even while both scenes show the certainty of divine victory.

The Final Destruction of Satan

Revelation 20:10 gives Satan's final end: "And the Devil who was deceiving them was hurled into the lake of fire and sulfur, where the beast and the false prophet already were; and they will be tormented day and night forever and ever." This is the climactic answer to the devil's entire career in Scripture. The serpent of Eden, the accuser of

Job, the dragon of Revelation, the deceiver of the whole inhabited earth, the power behind the beastly order, and the gatherer of the final rebellion is now cast into the same final judgment already assigned to the beast and false prophet.

The point of the passage is complete and irreversible judgment. Satan is not merely restrained now. He is removed forever from God's world. This is not the beginning of an eternal dualism in which evil continues as a rival kingdom to God. Revelation as a whole moves toward the complete abolition of evil, not its endless preservation as a conscious counter-order. The devil's judgment is final, public, and never reversed.

The language of torment day and night forever and ever must be read within the apocalyptic context and in harmony with the chapter's own interpretation of the lake of fire as the second death. The emphasis is on the absolute severity, public certainty, and irreversible nature of the judgment. Revelation's theological movement is toward the removal of rebellion from creation, not toward the eternal preservation of evil as an alternate realm. The devil's doom is complete. His deceiving work is over forever.

The Great White Throne

After the final rebellion is crushed and Satan is judged, Revelation 20:11-15 presents the great white throne: "And I saw a great white throne and the One seated on it. From before Him the earth and the heaven fled away, and no place was found for them." The throne is great because the judgment issuing from it is supreme and final. It is white because it is holy, pure, and incorruptible. This is not one tribunal among many. It is the last and ultimate court before which all remaining death-bound humanity is brought.

The statement that earth and heaven fled away from before the throne signifies the passing of the old order in preparation for final judgment. The present world-system in its old form has no lasting place before this throne. The old heaven and earth in their present arrangement are giving way so that the final judgment may clear the scene for the new heaven and new earth that follow in Revelation 21.

The image does not suggest that creation escapes God, but that the old order marred by sin, death, and curse is removed before the holiness of the final court.

This transition is important. Final judgment does not occur as a small event within ordinary history. It takes place at the threshold between the old order and the openly manifested new creation. Thus the great white throne belongs to the closing movement of God's kingdom purpose as it abolishes every remaining enemy and prepares the way for the new heaven and new earth.

The Dead Standing Before the Throne

Revelation 20:12 says, "And I saw the dead, the great and the small, standing before the throne, and scrolls were opened. But another scroll was opened; it is the scroll of life. And the dead were judged from the things written in the scrolls according to their deeds." This scene emphasizes universality and personal accountability. Great and small stand alike before the throne. Human rank, power, wealth, and obscurity mean nothing there. The court of God is impartial and exhaustive.

The opened scrolls signify the full divine record according to which judgment proceeds. Nothing is omitted or forgotten. The scroll of life introduces the decisive issue of final belonging. Judgment is therefore not arbitrary. It is precise, ordered, and morally exact. Deeds matter because they reveal what a person was in relation to God's truth and government. This does not teach salvation by works apart from God's grace and Christ's authority. Rather, it teaches that judgment deals with actual persons and actual lives. God's final court is not impressionistic. It is righteous.

Verse 13 adds, "And the sea gave up the dead in it, and death and Hades gave up the dead in them, and they were judged individually according to their deeds." No realm can keep the dead when God summons them. The sea, death, and Hades all yield their dead. Hades here must be understood as the grave, not a place of torment. It is emptied. The dead are brought forward. Then each is judged. The passage is universal and personal at once. No one is hidden in the mass. Every case is individual before God.

Death and Hades Destroyed

Revelation 20:14 then states, "And death and Hades were hurled into the lake of fire. This means the second death, the lake of fire." This is one of the most interpretively decisive statements in all of Revelation. Death and Hades are not personal moral agents. They are realities associated with the dead condition of mankind. Their being hurled into the lake of fire shows that the lake signifies final abolition and removal. Death itself is brought to an end. The grave has no future place in the new creation. The lake of fire is therefore identified as the second death.

That definition is crucial. The lake of fire is not another kind of life. It is the second death. The first death is the ordinary death from which there may be resurrection. The second death is the final death after judgment, from which there is no return. It is everlasting in result because it is irreversible. This is entirely consistent with the wider biblical language of destruction, Gehenna, annihilation, and the final removal of the wicked. Revelation itself defines the symbol, and that definition must govern interpretation.

This also means that the chapter's whole movement is toward abolition, not eternal preservation of death and evil. Death is destroyed. Hades is destroyed. Satan is removed. The beast and false prophet are already gone. The final rebellious nations are consumed. All not written in the scroll of life are hurled into the lake of fire, the second death. The chapter does not end with an eternal dualism of competing realms. It ends with the complete and irreversible removal of every death-bound and rebellious reality from God's order.

Those Not Found Written in the Scroll of Life

Revelation 20:15 concludes the chapter: "Furthermore, whoever was not found written in the scroll of life was hurled into the lake of fire." The scroll of life is therefore decisive. To be absent from it is to stand outside the life God grants and preserves. The lake of fire is the final judicial outcome for such persons. Again, because the text itself identifies the lake of fire as the second death, the final punishment is not everlasting life in misery, but final death in its irreversible form.

This keeps the chapter in harmony with the whole biblical witness. The wicked are destroyed. They perish. They are cut off. They go into second death. The righteous inherit life. The millennial administration of Christ moves toward the abolition of death itself. Therefore the final outcome of judgment is fully coherent: life for those approved by God, second death for those not written in the scroll of life, and no remaining realm in which death, rebellion, and the grave continue forever.

Book of Life: (βιβλου τῆς ζωῆς biblos tēs zōēs) In biblical times, cities had registered names for the citizens living there. (See Ps. 69:28; Isa. 4:3) God, figuratively speaking, has been writing names in the "book of life" "from the foundation of the world." (Rev. 17:8) Jesus Christ talked about Abel as living "from the foundation of the world," this would suggest that we are talking about the world of ransomable humankind after the fall. (Lu 11:48-51) Clearly, Abel was the first person to have his name written in the "book of life." The individuals whose names are written in the "book of Life" do not mean they are predestined to eternal life. This is evident from the fact that they can be 'blotted out' of the "book of life." (Ex 32:32-33; Rev. 3:5) Jesus' ransom sacrifice alone gets one written in the "book of life" if they accept the Son of God. However, it is remaining faithful to God that keeps them from being 'blotted' out of the "book of life." (Phil. 2:12; Heb. 10:26-27; Jam. 2:14-26) Only by remaining faithful until the end can one be retained permanently in the "book of life." – Matt. 214:13; Phil. 4:3; Rev. 20:15.

Theological Meaning of the Millennium

The millennium reveals several vital truths about God's kingdom. First, it shows that Christ's victory over the beastly order is not the end of kingdom administration but the beginning of a distinct phase in which the consequences of that victory are worked out under His rule. Second, it shows that Satan's power over the nations is not permanent. His deception can be shut down completely by heaven. Third, it shows that the faithful who conquered under the beast are not merely remembered but raised, enthroned, and given priestly-royal service with Christ. Fourth, it shows that even after a thousand years of kingdom administration, rebellion apart from God remains satanically rooted, which is why Satan's release immediately produces deception and revolt. Finally, it shows that God's kingdom does not merely restrain evil temporarily. It removes it finally.

The millennium therefore should not be treated as an optional side issue. It is the revealed kingdom era in which Christ's rule advances history toward final abolition of every enemy. It makes sense of the first resurrection, the binding of Satan, the later resurrection and judgment scenes, and the final disappearance of death. Without it, the sequence of Revelation 19–21 is flattened and much of the chapter's order is lost.

Living in Light of the Millennium and Final Judgment

The doctrine of the millennium, the final rebellion, and the great white throne is not given for speculation. It is given to teach how believers should see the present age and the certainty of God's future. The present beastly order is not permanent. Satan's deception is not ultimate. Faithfulness under pressure is not wasted. Death does not have the final word. The righteous are not forgotten. The wicked do not escape judgment. And the old order itself will not continue forever.

This doctrine also teaches humility. Even after the thousand years, once Satan is released, rebellion appears again wherever deception finds a hearing. This proves that apart from God's righteous rule and transforming truth, created beings do not sustain holiness by their own power. It also reveals the depth of satanic evil. The devil is not reformed by time, restrained by culture, or weakened into harmlessness by history alone. He remains the deceiver until his final destruction.

At the same time, the doctrine teaches assurance. Evil never threatens God on equal terms. The beast falls. Satan is bound. Gog and Magog are consumed by fire from heaven. The great white throne judges every remaining case with perfect righteousness. Death and Hades are destroyed. Nothing is unresolved when the new heaven and new earth appear. The kingdom of God does not leave loose ends in the moral government of the universe.

The Full Sequence of Revelation 20

When Revelation 20 is allowed to speak in its own order, the doctrine may be stated clearly. After Christ's visible return and His overthrow of the beast and false prophet, Satan is bound in the abyss for a literal thousand years so that he might not deceive the nations any longer. During that thousand years the faithful, beast-conquering company shares in the first resurrection, reigns with Christ, serves as priests of God and of Christ, and stands beyond the authority of the second death. After the thousand years Satan is released for a short time, deceives the nations once more, gathers Gog and Magog for the final rebellion, and is then forever removed when fire from heaven devours the rebels and the devil is cast into the lake of fire. After that comes the great white throne, where the remaining dead stand before God, are judged according to the scrolls and the scroll of life, and death and Hades themselves are abolished in the lake of fire, which is the second death.

This is the biblical structure. It preserves the premillennial order, the distinction of the first resurrection, the reality of the final rebellion, the certainty of the great white throne, and the final abolition of death. It also preserves the great hope that God's kingdom does not merely outlast evil. It judges, removes, and replaces it entirely.

The millennium, then, is the great kingdom era between the defeat of the present beastly order and the final abolition of death. The final rebellion is the last exposure of satanic deception after the thousand years. The great white throne is the final universal court in which every remaining death-bound case is brought under God's perfect judgment. Together these truths show that the reign of Christ is not symbolic idealism, but the real and ordered administration by which Jehovah brings all things to their appointed end and prepares the way for the new heaven and the new earth where righteousness is at home.

CHAPTER 13 Explaining the Final Judgment

The Nature of the Final Judgment

The final judgment is one of the most solemn and necessary doctrines in all of Scripture. It is necessary because the Bible does not present history as an endless cycle of human rebellion, partial reform, and unresolved moral chaos. Jehovah is the righteous Judge of all the earth, and He does not leave evil forever unexamined, unexposed, or unpunished. The final judgment is the public, universal, and irreversible session of divine justice by which every remaining death-bound case is brought under His perfect judgment through Jesus Christ, every unresolved moral account is answered, and all whose names are not found in the scroll of life pass into the second death. It is therefore not merely a religious symbol for accountability in general. It is the climactic judicial act by which God closes the old order and clears the way for the new heaven and new earth where righteousness is at home.

This doctrine must be understood in its proper biblical setting. The final judgment is not a vague process floating free of prophecy. It stands within the sequence of the last things. Christ returns in judgment against the beastly order. Satan is bound. The first-resurrection company reigns with Christ for the thousand years. Satan is then released for a short time, deceives the nations again, and the final rebellion is crushed. Only after these things does Revelation present the great white throne. The final judgment, then, is not identical with every prior act of judgment in history, nor is it merely another name for the whole reign of Christ. It is the last, universal judicial session following the destruction of Satan's final rebellion and preceding the open manifestation of the new creation.

The final judgment also must not be confused with the false idea that men naturally possess immortal souls already fixed in conscious bliss or torment. Scripture teaches that the dead are unconscious, that the grave is real, and that resurrection is necessary because death is real. Therefore final judgment includes resurrection. Those not already included in the first resurrection must be brought forward from death and Hades, from every realm that held them, and then judged according to God's righteous standards. The final judgment is thus inseparable from the resurrection hope. It is the judicial completion of Christ's triumph over death.

Jehovah as the Final Judge Through Christ

All judgment belongs ultimately to Jehovah, but Scripture also teaches plainly that He has entrusted judicial authority to His Son. Abraham's question remains foundational: "Will not the Judge of all the earth do what is right?" (Gen. 18:25). The Psalms celebrate Jehovah as the One who judges the peoples with uprightness and righteousness (Ps. 9:8; 96:13; 98:9). The prophets speak repeatedly of the Day of Jehovah as the time when He enters into judgment with the nations and vindicates His own name. Therefore the final judgment is first and foremost an act of Jehovah's holiness, justice, and sovereignty.

Yet the New Testament makes equally clear that this judgment is administered through Jesus Christ. Jesus says, "The Father judges no one at all, but He has entrusted all the judging to the Son" (John 5:22). He further says that the Father "has given Him authority to do judging, because He is the Son of man" (John 5:27). This means the final judgment is not detached from the person and work of Christ. The One who was rejected, crucified, and raised is the One through whom Jehovah will publicly judge mankind. The Judge is the risen Christ, acting in full obedience to the Father and in complete harmony with His righteousness.

Paul says that God "has set a day on which He purposes to judge the inhabited earth in righteousness by a man whom He has appointed, and He has furnished a guarantee to all men by resurrecting Him from the dead" (Acts 17:31). That statement is decisive. The resurrection of Jesus is not only the vindication of His Sonship. It is also God's public guarantee that final judgment will occur through Him. The same Christ who now reigns is the one by whom the last court is convened. This is why the doctrine of final judgment is profoundly Christological. It is not an impersonal process. It is the judicial act of Jehovah through the glorified Son.

Judgment in the Present and the Final Judgment Still to Come

Scripture speaks of judgment in more than one sense, and these distinctions must be preserved. There are historical judgments within history. Nations rise and fall under divine sentence. Individuals may come under forms of judgment now through the consequences of sin or through God's disciplinary acts. There is also the present judicial significance of one's response to Christ. Jesus says that the one not exercising faith "has been judged already" because he has not believed in the name of God's only-begotten Son (John 3:18). In this sense, men already place themselves in a judicial relation to God by how they respond to the truth in the present.

But these truths do not eliminate the future final judgment. Rather, they prepare for it. Present response to God matters because there is a last court in which all things are brought to light. The existence of present judgment does not mean that the final judgment has already occurred in full. The final judgment remains future, universal, public, and climactic. It belongs to the closing of this order and the transition to the new creation. The New Testament speaks plainly of "a day of judgment" (Matt. 10:15; 11:22, 24; 12:36), of "the day of wrath and of the revealing of God's righteous judgment" (Rom. 2:5), and of "judgment of a great day" for rebel angels (Jude 6). Therefore one must distinguish between anticipatory judgments now and the final judgment yet to come.

This distinction also helps guard against two opposite errors. One error is to think only of present moral consequences and deny the need for a future universal tribunal. The other is to think only of one future courtroom while neglecting the fact that one's response to God now already has judicial significance. Scripture teaches both. There is real accountability now, and there is a final judgment still to come.

The Great White Throne

The most direct and solemn description of the final judgment is Revelation 20:11-15. John writes, "And I saw a great white throne and the One seated on it. From before Him the earth and the heaven fled away, and no place was found for them. And I saw the dead, the great and the small, standing before the throne, and scrolls were opened. But another scroll was opened; it is the scroll of life. And the dead were judged from the things written in the scrolls according to their deeds" (Rev. 20:11-12). This is the final universal judicial scene after the destruction of Satan's final rebellion.

The throne is called great because the judgment issuing from it is supreme, final, and universal. It is called white because the judgment is holy, pure, and uncorrupted by any defect, bias, or injustice. No earthly court resembles it in authority. No appeal stands beyond it. This is the last court before which all remaining death-bound humanity must stand. Revelation has already shown the fall of Babylon, the destruction of the beast and false prophet, the binding of Satan, the thousand-year reign, the release of Satan, and the destruction of Gog and Magog. Now only one thing remains: the final adjudication of every unresolved human case before God.

The statement that earth and heaven flee away from before the throne means that the old order, as presently constituted under the shadow of sin, death, and curse, has no lasting place before this final judicial session. The image should not be treated as though creation somehow escapes God's presence. Rather, the point is that the old order in its present form is passing from the scene as final judgment is rendered and the way is prepared for the new heaven and new earth of Revelation 21. The final judgment therefore belongs to the end of the old order and to the transition into the openly manifested new creation.

The Dead, Great and Small, Standing Before the Throne

John sees "the dead, the great and the small" standing before the throne. This language emphasizes both universality and equality before divine justice. Human distinctions of rank, power, wealth, obscurity, prestige, and influence do not matter at the great white throne. Kings and servants, rulers and peasants, the learned and the simple, the celebrated and the forgotten all stand on the same ground before the Judge. There is no hiding in social status, and there is no escaping because of insignificance. Every remaining case comes under the same perfect scrutiny.

The dead standing before the throne also demonstrates once more that final judgment includes resurrection. The dead do not judge themselves, nor do they remain forever asleep in death without further divine dealing. They stand before the throne because Christ's authority has reached into death itself. Revelation 20:13 says that "the sea gave up the dead in it, and death and Hades gave up the dead in them." No realm can retain its dead when God summons them. The sea, which to human eyes may seem the most inaccessible place of death, gives up its dead. Death and Hades, the grave and the state of death, give up their dead. Thus the final judgment is universal because resurrection is universal in scope according to God's purpose.

This also means that the final judgment is not merely for those still living at Christ's return. It includes the dead. Those not in the first-resurrection company are brought forward in relation to this final judicial order. Here again resurrection and judgment are closely joined. If death were itself the final state in every sense, then no universal final judgment would be possible. But because God raises the dead, final judgment becomes the climactic expression of His justice over all mankind.

The Scrolls and the Scroll of Life

John says that scrolls were opened, and another scroll was opened, which is the scroll of life. These details are not incidental. The opened scrolls signify the full divine record according to which judgment proceeds. Nothing is forgotten, omitted, misremembered, or distorted. God's judgment is neither vague nor impressionistic. It deals with real persons and real deeds. The statement that "the dead were judged from the things written in the scrolls according to their deeds" shows that final judgment is historically concrete. Lives are not dissolved into abstraction. God's judgment takes account of what men actually were and did.

The scroll of life introduces another essential dimension. Judgment is not only by record but also by relation to divine life. The scroll of life signifies those who belong to God in the final sense. Revelation repeatedly speaks of names written in the scroll of life in relation to those who belong to the Lamb and are not finally lost. Therefore final judgment is not simply a matter of isolated deeds considered apart from God's redemptive purpose. It includes the decisive issue of whether one stands written in the scroll of life. The opened scrolls reveal the moral history of each life. The scroll of life reveals the final issue of divine acceptance unto life.

These two realities must be held together. Scripture never allows moral accountability to be erased. Men are judged according to deeds. At the same time, life belongs to God and to the Lamb. The final judgment therefore reveals both perfect justice and the decisive importance of standing in relation to the life God gives. No one drifts accidentally into life. No one escapes the truth of his deeds. And no one can challenge the righteousness of the verdict rendered at the throne.

According to Their Deeds

The repeated statement that each is judged "according to their deeds" requires careful attention. It does not teach that men earn life by works apart from God's grace or apart from Christ's authority. Rather, it teaches that final judgment is morally exact. God judges persons as they truly are. Deeds reveal the shape of a life, the response of the heart, and the reality of one's standing before divine truth. This principle is taught throughout Scripture. Jesus says men will render an account for every unprofitable saying on Judgment Day (Matt. 12:36). Paul says God "will repay to each one according to his works" (Rom. 2:6). Second Corinthians 5:10 says, "We must all be made manifest before the judgment seat of the Christ, so that each one may get his award for the things done through the body, according to the things he has practiced, whether good or vile."

This means final judgment is neither arbitrary nor purely formal. It is not merely the announcement of a status disconnected from the actual course of life. God's judgment answers to reality. For the righteous, deeds confirm the life of faith, loyalty, and obedience under the light they had received. For the unrighteous, deeds become part of the judicial assessment under Christ's administration. For the wicked, deeds expose settled rebellion and justify final destruction. The formula "according to their deeds" is therefore not opposed to grace rightly understood. It is opposed to every idea that God judges blindly, carelessly, or without moral truth.

This also preserves the seriousness of human action. What men do matters. What they say matters. What they embrace, resist, or become matters. History is not morally neutral in the presence of God. Every deed belongs to the final court, and every life is opened before Him.

The Righteous, the Unrighteous, and the Wicked in the Final Judgment

The doctrine of final judgment must preserve the distinctions Scripture itself gives. As earlier passages show, there is a resurrection of the righteous and the unrighteous (Acts 24:15). The righteous are those approved by Jehovah, those whose resurrection belongs to life. The unrighteous are those not counted as righteous servants in their former life, yet still raised into divine judicial administration rather than simply ignored. The wicked are the finally condemned rebels whose end is second death.

This distinction matters deeply in the final judgment. The righteous do not stand before the throne as those uncertain whether God remembers them or as those entering a morally unformed process. Their standing is one of divine favor. For the blessed and holy who share in the first resurrection, the second death has no authority at all (Rev. 20:6). Their role in Christ's kingdom has already been established. For the broader righteous, final judgment confirms the gift of life under God's kingdom. Their names are in the scroll of life, and their deeds accord with a life of covenant loyalty.

The unrighteous, however, stand in a different relation to judgment. Their resurrection is associated with judgment in the sense of divine assessment and accountability. They are not to be carelessly collapsed into the finally wicked. Scripture's inclusion of them in resurrection means that Jehovah's judicial administration is broader than simple immediate destruction for all who were not righteous in their former life. Yet neither are they automatically life-approved apart from divine evaluation. The final judgment therefore gives full weight to deeds, accountability, and the scroll of life in determining outcome under Christ's righteous rule.

The wicked are a distinct class. Scripture associates them with destruction, Gehenna, the second death, and everlasting abhorrence. Their end is not preservation in torment, but irreversible destruction under divine judgment. The final judgment thus reveals the full moral distinction among men and issues in final outcomes appropriate to God's perfect justice.

Death and Hades Hurled Into the Lake of Fire

One of the most decisive statements in the passage is Revelation 20:14: "And death and Hades were hurled into the lake of fire. This means the second death, the lake of fire." This verse interprets the symbol. The lake of fire is the second death. Because death and Hades are not personal moral agents but realities associated with the dead condition of mankind, their being cast into the lake of fire shows that the symbol signifies abolition and final removal. Death itself is brought to an end. The grave is emptied and abolished. There is no future for Hades, no future for death, and no further place for the old order of mortality in the new creation.

This has major doctrinal importance. It means the final judgment does not end with the endless preservation of death in another form. It ends with death's destruction. The first death is the ordinary death inherited through Adam, from which resurrection is possible. The second death is the final death after judgment, from which there is no resurrection and no return. It is death in its judicial finality. This is why the lake of fire must not be redefined as endless conscious life in torment. Revelation itself calls it death—second death. The symbol is severe because the finality is severe. But the text's own interpretation must govern.

This also harmonizes with the wider biblical witness. The wicked are annihilated, cut off, destroyed, and removed. The last enemy, death, is abolished. The universe does not remain forever divided between life in God's kingdom and life in endless torment. Rather, death and the grave are themselves destroyed, and all not written in the scroll of life are consigned to the same final removal.

The Final Judgment and the Character of God

The final judgment reveals the full harmony of Jehovah's justice, holiness, wisdom, and love. His justice appears because no evil is ignored, no rebellion is treated lightly, and every deed is weighed in truth. His holiness appears because the great white throne is pure, the old defiled order flees from before it, and nothing unclean passes into the new creation. His wisdom appears because the whole sequence of kingdom, resurrection, final rebellion, and judgment is perfectly ordered. His love appears not in the absence of judgment, but in the fact that His purpose in Christ reaches beyond the grave, that life is granted through His Son, and that evil is removed rather than allowed to wound His creation forever.

The false doctrine of eternal torment often distorts the character of God by portraying Him as eternally preserving the wicked in conscious agony. Scripture does not teach that. It teaches final judgment, second death, and irreversible destruction. That doctrine is severe enough because it is final, but it does not make God the perpetual sustainer of a universe in which evil survives forever in another form. Instead, the final judgment clears the way for the complete abolition of death, pain, curse, and rebellion.

The Final Judgment Clears the Way for the New Creation

The final judgment is not the end of God's purpose. It is the necessary clearing of the old order so that the new may be openly established. Revelation 21 follows immediately with the new heaven and new earth, the holy city, the dwelling of God with mankind, and the removal of death, mourning, outcry, and pain. This order matters. The final judgment removes what cannot remain in the new creation. The scrolls are opened, names are assessed in relation to the scroll of life, death and Hades are abolished, and all not found written in the scroll of life pass into the second death. Then the new creation appears in its unveiled glory.

This means the final judgment is not merely negative. It is deeply hopeful for the righteous because it guarantees that evil will not persist indefinitely. The righteous are not merely spared. They enter a world fully cleansed by divine judgment. The kingdom of God does not tolerate unresolved rebellion forever. It judges, removes, and replaces the old order with the new.

This also helps explain why final judgment is necessary even after the millennium and after the destruction of Satan's final rebellion. The moral universe must be publicly and finally set right. Every remaining death-bound case must be answered. Every realm that held the dead must be emptied. Every unresolved name must be brought into relation with the scroll of life. Only then is the victory of God over death and rebellion complete in public form.

Living in Light of the Final Judgment

The doctrine of the final judgment is not given for speculation but for seriousness, holiness, humility, and hope. It teaches that life now matters because deeds matter. It teaches that one cannot hide behind human greatness or insignificance, because both great and small stand before the throne. It teaches that death is not escape from accountability, because death and Hades give up their dead. It teaches that the wicked do not finally prevail, because second death awaits those not found in the scroll of life. And it teaches that the righteous need not fear that evil will persist forever, because the final judgment abolishes death itself.

This doctrine should also produce reverence toward Christ. The Judge is the One who died and rose. He is the One who now holds authority over life and judgment. To respond rightly to Him now is to live in the light of the coming court. To ignore Him is to move toward that court unprepared. The final judgment therefore presses the gospel upon the conscience. The One who judges is also the One through whom Jehovah provides life.

The Full Doctrine of the Final Judgment

When the biblical witness is brought together, the doctrine may be stated plainly. The final judgment is the last universal judicial session of Jehovah through Jesus Christ, taking place after the thousand-year reign and after the destruction of Satan's final rebellion. At the great white throne the old order flees, the dead are summoned from every realm that held them, the scrolls and the scroll of life are opened, and each one is judged according to his deeds. The righteous are confirmed in life, the unrighteous stand under divine judicial determination according to God's perfect justice, and all not found written in the scroll of life pass into the second death. Death and Hades themselves are abolished in the lake of fire. Thus the final judgment ends not in the endless preservation of evil, but in its complete and irreversible removal.

This is the fitting climax of biblical eschatology. It answers every accusation that history ends in moral confusion. It answers every fear that the grave has the last word. It answers every illusion that evil can survive alongside God's kingdom forever. And it prepares the way for the new heaven and new earth where death is no more, the curse is removed, and God dwells with mankind in righteousness. The final judgment, then, is terrible in its holiness, perfect in its justice, and hopeful in its outcome, because through it Jehovah by means of His Christ removes the last remnants of the old rebellious order and opens the fully cleansed world of everlasting life.

CHAPTER 14 Explaining the Unevangelized

The Question of the Unevangelized

The question of the unevangelized is one of the most serious and emotionally weighty questions in all theology. It asks what becomes of those who died without receiving a full witness to the good news, without understanding the truth clearly, or without a fair opportunity to respond to the revelation God has given in Christ. It is a question that touches the justice of Jehovah, the necessity of Christ, the reality of judgment, the meaning of evangelism, and the scope of the resurrection hope. Because it is such a sensitive question, men often answer it by instinct, sentiment, or inherited tradition rather than by careful attention to the wording and flow of Scripture. Yet the matter must be handled biblically, because only the revealed Word of God can protect the church from both cruelty and confusion.

Two opposite errors commonly appear. One error says that all who die without hearing the gospel are automatically lost forever, as though Jehovah were indifferent to the actual light available to them and as though death outside explicit knowledge of Christ settled every case identically. The other error says that all the unevangelized are automatically saved, as though ignorance itself were righteousness and as though the need for repentance, judgment, and response to God no longer mattered. Scripture supports neither extreme. The Bible does not portray Jehovah as unjust, and it does not present Him as morally indifferent. He judges according to truth, according to light, according to deeds, and according to His own righteous standards. At the same time, He has appointed His Son as the Life-Giver and Judge, and He will deal with mankind under an ordered kingdom administration that reaches beyond the grave.

This means the doctrine of the unevangelized must be framed within the whole biblical structure of death, resurrection, judgment, and the kingdom of Christ. It cannot be answered correctly if man is thought to possess an immortal soul that goes immediately to fixed bliss or torment at death. It cannot be answered correctly if resurrection is neglected. And it cannot be answered correctly if the categories of the righteous, the unrighteous, and the wicked are collapsed into one flat moral class. Scripture requires more care than that. It presents a resurrection of the righteous and the unrighteous, a final destruction of the wicked, and a kingdom order in which Christ's judicial administration reaches beyond the grave. The unevangelized belong within that framework.

The Character of Jehovah as the Starting Point

The starting point for any answer must be the character of Jehovah. The question of the unevangelized is not first solved by human feeling, but neither is it solved by a cold formula detached from who God is. Scripture reveals Jehovah as righteous in all His ways and loyal in all His works (Ps. 145:17). Abraham's question remains permanently relevant: "Will not the Judge of all the earth do what is right?" (Gen. 18:25). The implied answer is yes. Jehovah never acts with injustice. He is never arbitrary. He does not punish the innocent as guilty, nor does He confuse ignorance with rebellion. His judgments are true and righteous altogether.

This is especially important because religious systems have often portrayed God in ways that make the conscience recoil. If one imagines that countless millions who never heard the name of Christ, never had access to Scripture, never received fair instruction, and never consciously rejected the gospel are automatically consigned to irreversible punishment in the same sense as hardened God-haters, the justice of God is obscured. Scripture does not permit such a careless doctrine. Jehovah is not a tribal deity protecting a narrow information boundary. He is the Creator of all mankind, the God who formed every nation, appointed their seasons and boundaries, and who knows the secrets of every heart.

At the same time, His justice does not mean that ignorance is itself saving righteousness. He is also holy. He does not lower His moral standards into indifference. The fact that He judges rightly does not imply that men may live apart from truth and never answer for what they were or how they walked according to the light available to them. Therefore the doctrine of the unevangelized must be held between two certainties: Jehovah will never judge unjustly, and Jehovah will never treat evil as unimportant. Both truths stand together in Scripture, and both must govern the discussion.

Christ Is the Only Ground of Salvation

A biblical doctrine of the unevangelized must also preserve the unique role of Jesus Christ. The question is not whether some are saved apart from Him. Scripture gives no room for that idea. Jesus says, "I am the way and the truth and the life. No one comes to the Father except through me" (John 14:6). Peter declares, "There is no salvation in anyone else, for there is no other name under heaven that has been given among men by which we must get saved" (Acts 4:12). Paul says there is "one God, and one mediator between God and men, a man, Christ Jesus, who gave Himself a corresponding ransom for all" (1 Tim. 2:5-6).

This means that no doctrine of the unevangelized may suggest that men are saved by ignorance, by natural virtue alone, or by some independent path outside Christ. If any unevangelized person finally receives life, that life still comes through the ransom, authority, and kingdom administration of Jesus Christ. There is no other mediator, no other basis of reconciliation, and no other resurrection hope. The issue, then, is not whether Christ may be bypassed, but how His mediatorial work and His judicial authority apply to those who died without a fair and full opportunity to know Him.

This is where many discussions go wrong. They assume only two options: either a person explicitly hears and responds now, or he is forever lost. But Scripture presents a broader kingdom framework. Christ is not only Savior in the present proclamation of the gospel. He is also Judge, Resurrection, and King. His authority reaches into death itself. All in the memorial tombs hear His voice. There is a resurrection of the righteous and the unrighteous. Therefore the question is not confined to what men did or did not know before death in isolation. It must be asked in relation to the full scope of Christ's judicial and life-giving office.

General Revelation and Human Accountability

Before turning to resurrection, it is necessary to consider what Scripture says about human accountability even before the gospel reaches a person explicitly. Paul says in Romans 1:19-20 that what may be known about God is evident among men, because God made it evident to them, and that His invisible qualities are clearly seen from the world's creation onward, because they are perceived by the things made, so that men are inexcusable. This passage shows that mankind is not morally blank simply because special revelation is absent. Creation itself bears witness to God's existence, power, and divinity. Therefore no one can claim absolute innocence in the sense that he lived in a universe giving no testimony at all to its Maker.

Paul continues in Romans 2 by speaking of Gentiles who do not have the Law but "do by nature the things of the Law," showing "the matter of the law written in their hearts," while their conscience bears witness and their thoughts accuse or even excuse them (Rom. 2:14-16). This is a very important text for the unevangelized. It does not teach salvation by conscience or by natural morality apart from God. But it does teach that accountability is measured in relation to actual moral knowledge and conscience, not merely external possession of written revelation. God judges the secrets of mankind through Christ Jesus. That means His judgment reaches beneath outward circumstance to the actual state of the person in relation to the light available.

This point protects against crude simplifications. The unevangelized are not morally blank, yet neither are they judged as though they had all the privileges and light of those who received clear revelation and then trampled it. Scripture insists both on human accountability and on proportional justice. Jesus says it will be more tolerable for some cities than for others in the day of judgment because greater light had been given to some than to others (Matt. 11:20-24). This principle of greater light bringing greater accountability is essential. It means that Jehovah's judgment is not flat. He knows what each person actually knew, resisted, desired, practiced, and would respond to under His righteous administration.

The Righteous, the Unrighteous, and the Wicked

The biblical categories must now be stated clearly. Scripture distinguishes the righteous, the unrighteous, and the wicked. These are not interchangeable terms. If they are merged carelessly, the doctrine of the unevangelized immediately becomes confused.

The righteous are those approved by Jehovah. They are those who lived in covenant loyalty according to the light and responsibility given them. Their resurrection belongs to life. Daniel 12:2 speaks of some awakening to everlasting life. Jesus speaks of those who did good things coming out to a resurrection of life (John 5:29). Paul affirms a resurrection of the righteous (Acts 24:15). Their final outcome is favorable because they belong to God in faith and obedience.

The unrighteous are different. Paul still includes them in the resurrection hope when he speaks of "a resurrection both of the righteous and the unrighteous" (Acts 24:15). This category must not be erased. The unrighteous are not presented as righteous servants of Jehovah, yet neither are they automatically identified with the finally wicked. They include those who did not live as approved covenant servants and often those who lacked a fair opportunity for full knowledge, instruction, or accountable response to divine truth. Their resurrection is associated with judgment, not with automatic life, but also not with immediate automatic final destruction in the same way as the wicked.

The wicked are those who stand in settled, culpable, and final rebellion against Jehovah. Scripture speaks of their end as destruction, Gehenna, second death, and everlasting abhorrence. They are not portrayed as a class raised for rehabilitation under the kingdom. Their end is irreversible removal. This distinction is vital. Not all who are unrighteous are therefore wicked in the final, settled, and irredeemable sense. Scripture's categories are more precise than many theological systems allow.

The unevangelized, therefore, generally belong not to the category of the righteous if they did not knowingly live in covenant loyalty to Jehovah, and not necessarily to the category of the finally wicked merely because they lacked a full gospel witness. They stand most naturally within the category of the unrighteous who are raised into judgment under Christ's administration.

The Resurrection of the Unevangelized

Acts 24:15 is one of the most important verses in the subject: "There is going to be a resurrection both of the righteous and the unrighteous." Paul's wording is plain, and it must be allowed to speak with its full force. The unevangelized are not excluded from resurrection merely because they died without hearing the good news fully. If they are not among the righteous, then they belong within the unrighteous class, and Paul explicitly says that this class is included in resurrection.

Jesus' words in John 5:28-29 harmonize with this. "The hour is coming in which all those in the memorial tombs will hear His voice and come out, those who did good things to a resurrection of life, those who practiced vile things to a resurrection of judgment." Here again the distinction between life and judgment must be preserved. Jesus does not say that all who are not already righteous are excluded from resurrection. He says some come out to life and others to judgment. This fits precisely with the category Paul names as the unrighteous. They are not raised as though already approved unto everlasting life, but neither are they thereby excluded from the resurrection program. They are raised into Christ's judicial administration.

This is one of the most important correctives in the whole discussion. Many theological systems assume that death fixes all human beings into two immediate and final states without remainder. But the biblical doctrine of resurrection does not allow that simplification. The dead are raised. Some are righteous and come into life. Others are unrighteous and come into judgment. The final wicked, by contrast, are associated with irreversible destruction. Therefore the unevangelized should be discussed primarily within the category of the unrighteous, not outside resurrection hope altogether.

This does not mean the unevangelized are automatically safe simply because they lacked information. It means they are not beyond the reach of Christ's judicial kingdom. Death does not settle their case in the same way it settles the case of those finally judged as wicked. Christ's authority extends into the grave, and the resurrection of the unrighteous is itself a testimony that Jehovah's justice and mercy operate in an ordered way beyond death.

The Meaning of a Resurrection of Judgment

The phrase "resurrection of judgment" in John 5:29 requires careful explanation. It is often assumed to mean resurrection only for immediate re-condemnation. But the term judgment, as used in Scripture, can include assessment, examination, decision, and the process by which a person is brought under righteous determination. This is especially clear when John 5 is read in harmony with Acts 24:15.

If the unrighteous are raised, and if they are not identical with the finally wicked, then their resurrection to judgment must include divine judicial evaluation under Christ's kingdom rule.

This is not leniency, and it is not universalism. Judgment remains serious, moral, and decisive. The point is that the unrighteous are raised into a condition where they stand under the righteous standards of Jehovah as administered by Christ. Their resurrection is therefore not simply a mechanical event preceding immediate destruction. It is resurrection into the sphere where divine truth, kingdom rule, and accountable response determine final outcome.

This is also consistent with the larger kingdom structure. Christ reigns for a thousand years. The first-resurrection company reigns with Him as priests and kings. The kingdom is not a passive interval. It is a period of active administration, judgment, and the progressive bringing of all things into subjection to God's purpose. Therefore it is entirely in harmony with Scripture that the unrighteous, including the unevangelized, are brought under this administration in a resurrection of judgment. Their future is not decided by human speculation, but by the perfect justice of the enthroned Christ.

Why the Unevangelized Are Not Automatically Condemned as the Wicked

A crucial distinction must be maintained here. The wicked are not merely those who died without hearing. The wicked are those who stand in settled, culpable hostility toward Jehovah, persisting in rebellion to the point of irreversible condemnation. Scripture uses severe language for them: destruction, second death, Gehenna, and everlasting abhorrence. Their end is final removal. They are not presented as the beneficiaries of restorative resurrection hope.

The unevangelized, however, cannot be carelessly placed in this category merely because they lacked a full witness. To do so would ignore the biblical principle of judgment according to light and accountability. Jesus explicitly says it will be more tolerable for some than for others in the day of judgment because of the differing degrees of light received and rejected (Matt. 11:20-24). That principle is not a minor detail. It reveals the moral structure of divine judgment. Greater light brings greater accountability. Lesser light does not erase accountability, but it does affect the justice of the case.

This means that those who died without hearing the gospel clearly, without understanding the truth fully, or without a fair opportunity to respond to Christ are not rightly treated as though they consciously and knowingly rejected the same witness given to those who heard and opposed it. Jehovah knows the actual condition of each heart, the actual knowledge each person possessed, the conscience each one violated or followed, and the way each one would stand under the revelation of His kingdom. Therefore the unevangelized are not outside judgment, but neither are they to be treated as the finally wicked by a crude theological shortcut.

Why the Unevangelized Are Not Automatically Saved Either

Yet Scripture equally forbids the opposite mistake. Ignorance is not righteousness. Lack of explicit gospel knowledge is not the same as covenant loyalty to Jehovah. Romans 1 shows that all men receive some witness from creation itself. Romans 2 shows that conscience also bears witness. Therefore the unevangelized are not a morally innocent class in the absolute sense. They are still sinners descending from Adam. They still die because sin reigns in mankind. They still require the ransom of Christ, and they still require God's judicial mercy if they are ever to live.

This is why the Bible never says, "Blessed are the ignorant, for ignorance saves." Rather, it says that salvation is through Christ and that judgment is according to truth. The unevangelized are not automatically justified because they lacked a full witness. They stand in need of Christ as truly as those who heard the gospel directly. If they receive life, it will be because Christ's ransom, authority, and kingdom administration have been applied to them in accordance with Jehovah's justice.

This point protects the urgency of evangelism. If ignorance guaranteed life, then preaching the gospel would become a tragic danger rather than a blessing, because it would expose men to greater accountability who were safer without it. Scripture never reasons this way. The good news is genuinely good news. The command to preach to all nations is not a divine trap. The gospel is life-giving truth now. At the same time, the fact that evangelism is necessary does not mean those unreached are automatically fixed in the same category as hardened rejecters. Scripture is more precise than either extreme.

The Kingdom Administration and the Unevangelized

The doctrine of the unevangelized becomes far clearer when placed within the kingdom administration of Christ. Jesus is not only the One who saves those who hear and respond now. He is also the One who raises the dead, judges the secrets of men, and reigns until all enemies are placed under His feet. This means the question of the unevangelized cannot be answered only by asking what happened before death. It must also be asked in relation to what Christ does after death in resurrection and judgment.

Revelation 20 shows the first-resurrection company reigning with Christ during the thousand years. Acts 24:15 shows a resurrection of the righteous and the unrighteous. John 5:28-29 shows that all in the memorial tombs hear Christ's voice and come out, some to life and some to judgment. Taken together, these passages indicate that the kingdom reign of Christ is the sphere in which resurrection and judgment are brought to completion. The unevangelized, as part of the unrighteous, stand under that administration.

This does not mean that the kingdom is a second chance offered in the careless sense often imagined by human sentiment. Scripture does not present resurrection as a trivial reset button. Resurrection is serious. Judgment is serious. Christ's rule is righteous, not indulgent. The point is not that the unevangelized are guaranteed favorable outcome later. The point is that Jehovah has not left their case outside the reach of His ordered judicial kingdom. They are not saved by ignorance, but neither are they judged by man's crude formulas. They are brought under the rule of the One appointed as Judge and Life-Giver.

The Unevangelized and the Great White Throne

The final judicial scene of Revelation 20:11-15 gives further clarity. John sees the dead, great and small, standing before the throne. The scrolls are opened. The scroll of life is opened. The dead are judged according to their deeds. Death and Hades give up the dead in them. No realm can keep its dead when the throne of God summons them. This scene shows that the final judgment is universal, personal, and morally exact. It also shows that death itself does not settle every case in advance in the sense some systems claim. The dead are raised and judged.

The unevangelized clearly belong within the kind of people envisioned here. They are among the dead given up by death and Hades. Their case is not ignored, and it is not handled outside the throne of God. Their deeds matter. The light they had matters. Their response to conscience matters. Their place in relation to the scroll of life matters. Every human life is brought into exact relation to divine judgment.

This should produce both sobriety and confidence. Sobriety, because the unevangelized are not outside judgment and cannot be spoken of lightly as though ignorance itself were salvation. Confidence, because their case is not lost in the machinery of death or in the ignorance of human systems. The final Judge knows what man does not know. He knows the heart, the conscience, the light, the motives, and the actual moral shape of each life. Therefore the unevangelized are safest, not in human theories, but in the justice of Jehovah through Christ.

The Hopeful Force of Acts 24:15

Acts 24:15 deserves special emphasis because it is one of the few places where the resurrection of the unrighteous is stated so plainly.

Paul says he has hope toward God that there is going to be a resurrection both of the righteous and the unrighteous. This is hope. He does not frame it as a terrifying concession. He frames it as part of his hope toward God. That does not mean every unrighteous person will finally receive life. But it does mean that the resurrection of the unrighteous is part of the hopeful structure of God's kingdom purpose rather than a bare declaration of hopelessness.

This is especially relevant for the unevangelized. They are not beyond hope merely because their earthly life ended without full gospel knowledge. The resurrection of the unrighteous means that Jehovah's purpose in Christ reaches beyond the grave in a way that includes those not counted among the righteous in their former life. That alone should restrain all dogmatic declarations that the unevangelized are simply and automatically lost.

At the same time, Acts 24:15 must not be turned into sentimental certainty that all such persons will finally live. Paul's hope is tied to God's order of resurrection and judgment, not to indifference about righteousness. The verse opens the door Scripture opens, and it closes the door Scripture closes. It opens the door of resurrection hope for the unrighteous. It does not close the door of judgment, accountability, and final destruction for those who prove wicked under God's righteous administration.

Why Evangelism Still Matters

Some may ask whether this doctrine weakens the urgency of evangelism. It does not. In fact, it protects evangelism from becoming distorted by false alternatives. Evangelism matters because Christ commanded it. The good news of the kingdom must be preached in all the inhabited earth for a witness to all the nations (Matt. 24:14). Men need truth now. They need repentance now. They need forgiveness now. They need to become disciples now. To know Christ now is blessing, not danger.

Evangelism also matters because greater light means greater accountability, but it also means greater opportunity for covenant loyalty, present peace with God, and faithful participation in His purpose. Scripture never treats ignorance as a better condition than knowledge. It treats ignorance as deficiency, darkness, and a condition in need of truth. The fact that Jehovah judges the unevangelized justly does not mean it is better for men to remain unevangelized. It means that the Judge will not act unjustly toward those who were not reached.

Furthermore, evangelism has to do with more than escaping future destruction. It is about bringing men into worship of the true God, obedience to His Word, fellowship with His people, and present hope in Christ. The kingdom message changes lives now. Therefore the doctrine of the unevangelized should never be used to cool zeal for preaching. It should instead give confidence that Jehovah's justice is not dependent on human evangelistic success in a mechanical way, even while His command to preach remains binding and urgent.

The Unevangelized and Children, Ignorance, and Mental Limitation

The question of the unevangelized often overlaps with questions about children, those with severe mental limitation, and those whose circumstances never allowed meaningful understanding. Scripture does not provide a single formula naming each such case individually, but the principles already established apply with great force. Jehovah judges according to truth. He knows the degree of knowledge, capacity, and accountability in every life. He is not deceived by appearances, and He is never unjust.

This means that those who lacked not only opportunity but capacity for meaningful accountable response are certainly not hidden from His understanding. The same God who formed the spirit of man within him knows perfectly what each life did or did not have in the way of moral comprehension. Therefore such cases should be left, not to hard dogmatism, but to the righteousness and mercy of Jehovah as exercised through Christ's judicial authority.

Again, this does not mean human beings may invent promises God has not explicitly stated. But it does mean that the church must not go beyond Scripture in severity. The final Judge knows what men do not know, and the resurrection of the unrighteous shows that His dealings are broader and more ordered than human systems often allow.

The Final Limits of Hope

Though the doctrine of the unevangelized is hopeful, it is not limitless in the sentimental sense. Scripture does set final boundaries. There is a class called wicked. There is Gehenna. There is the second death. There are those who refuse God in settled rebellion. There is final destruction from which there is no return. Therefore the doctrine of the unevangelized must never be turned into a denial of final judgment or into a universal restoration theory. The Bible does not teach that all finally live. It teaches that all come under God's justice, and that His kingdom extends beyond the grave in an ordered way.

This is why the distinction between the unrighteous and the wicked is so important. The unevangelized belong naturally under the former category, not the latter, unless their life actually manifested that settled and culpable wickedness known fully to God. This allows hope without denying final destruction. It preserves mercy without abolishing justice. It keeps Christ central without making present evangelism meaningless.

The Best Biblical Conclusion

When all the relevant passages are taken together, the best biblical conclusion is clear. The unevangelized are not automatically saved, because salvation is through Christ alone, ignorance is not righteousness, and all men remain accountable according to the light they had. But the unevangelized are not automatically condemned as though lack of a fair witness made no difference before the Judge of all the earth. Scripture distinguishes the righteous, the unrighteous, and the wicked. It promises a resurrection of both the righteous and the unrighteous. It teaches that the dead are judged according to their deeds, according to light, and under the authority of Christ.

Therefore the unevangelized belong most naturally within the category of the unrighteous who are raised into judgment under

Christ's kingdom administration. Their final outcome is not decided by human speculation, but by Jehovah's perfect justice through the One He has appointed as Judge and Life-Giver. If they attain life, it will be only through Christ. If they are condemned, it will be with perfect righteousness, never with cruelty or arbitrariness. The church may therefore reject both harsh dogmatism and sentimental universalism. It may say with confidence that Jehovah will do what is right, that Christ's kingdom reaches beyond the grave, and that no unevangelized person is lost in the ignorance of man or outside the knowledge of God.

The doctrine of the unevangelized, then, is not a doctrine of certainty without judgment, nor a doctrine of judgment without hope. It is a doctrine of resurrection, kingdom administration, and perfect justice. It reminds the faithful that Jehovah is never unjust, that Christ's mediatorial work is the only ground of life, that the grave is not beyond His reach, and that the final answer to this question lies not in human systems but in the righteous throne of God. That answer is enough, because the Judge of all the earth will indeed do what is right.

CHAPTER 15 Explaining the New Heavens and New Earth

The expression "new heavens and new earth" stands among the most hope-filled declarations in all of Scripture. It gathers into one phrase the end of rebellion, the removal of death, the vindication of God's people, the cleansing of creation, and the permanent establishment of Jehovah's righteous rule. In Revelation 21:1 John writes, "Then I saw a new heaven and a new earth, for the first heaven and the first earth had passed away, and the sea was no more." This is not a minor revision of the old order. It is the climactic renewal that follows the final judgment described in Revelation 20. The old order, marked by sin, corruption, oppression, pain, and death, gives way to an order entirely suited to Jehovah's holiness and purpose. The point is not merely that conditions improve. The point is that God brings into being the enduring order in which righteousness dwells, exactly as He promised beforehand through the prophets.

The background for John's language reaches deeply into the Old Testament. Isaiah 65:17 records Jehovah's promise: "For behold, I create new heavens and a new earth, and the former things shall not be remembered or come into mind." Isaiah 66:22 adds, "For as the new heavens and the new earth that I make shall remain before me, says Jehovah, so shall your offspring and your name remain." These prophetic words establish that the new creation is not an afterthought. It belongs to Jehovah's long-announced purpose. He did not create the earth to surrender it forever to wickedness, nor did He form mankind so that death would have the last word. Ecclesiastes 1:4 says, "A generation goes, and a generation comes, but the earth remains forever." Psalm 37:29 declares, "The righteous shall inherit the land and dwell upon it forever." Accordingly, the new earth must be understood as the restored and fully ordered sphere in which redeemed human life continues under God's blessing, free from all the defilements that belonged to the former order.

The Meaning of New in the New Creation

The word "new" in Revelation 21 does not mean new merely in the sense of recent. It carries the thought of renewal, transformation, and the bringing in of a different order suited to Jehovah's completed purpose. Scripture often uses "new" to describe not merely something later in time, but something superior in quality, purified from what was defective, and established according to God's will. Thus the new covenant is not simply the next covenant chronologically. It is the covenantal arrangement that brings God's redemptive purpose to its intended fulfillment through Christ. In the same way, the new heavens and new earth are the perfected order that replaces the old as it stood under the curse of sin and death.

Second Peter 3:10-13 is crucial here. Peter writes that "the day of the Lord will come like a thief, and then the heavens will pass away with a roar, and the heavenly bodies will be burned up and dissolved." He then adds in verse 13, "But according to his promise we are waiting for new heavens and a new earth in which righteousness dwells." Peter's emphasis is moral and theological. The present order as dominated by rebellion cannot remain. The future order is characterized by righteousness. The contrast is not between material existence and non-existence, but between a world under corruption and a world fully purged and ordered under Jehovah's will. The passing away of the former heavens and earth means the end of the old system of things in its sinful, death-governed condition. The new heavens and new earth are the sphere in which that entire condition has been removed.

This is why Revelation 21 must never be reduced to a vague symbol for "going to heaven." John does not say that redeemed humanity finally abandons created existence. He says that he saw a new heaven and a new earth, and then he sees the holy city coming down out of heaven from God. The movement is downward, not upward. The final hope is not escape from creation, but creation brought into perfect harmony with its Creator. Romans 8:19-23 supports this understanding. Paul teaches that the creation itself has been subjected to futility because of man's fall, but that it will be set free from its bondage to corruption. The destiny of creation is not perpetual ruin. Its destiny is liberation through God's redemptive purpose.

The Passing Away of the Former Heavens and Earth

John says that "the first heaven and the first earth had passed away." That expression requires careful attention. It does not teach that God's original creative purpose failed and had to be discarded. Rather, it teaches that the order of things as marked by sin, curse, Satanic deception, and death has come to its appointed end. Revelation has already shown the downfall of Babylon, the destruction of the beast and the false prophet, the binding and final doom of Satan, the resurrection of the dead, and the great white throne judgment. Once those events are completed, the old order has no further place.

The language of passing away appears elsewhere in Scripture to describe the removal of a present condition and the arrival of a divinely ordained replacement. First John 2:17 says, "The world is passing away along with its desires, but whoever does the will of God abides forever." The "world" there is not the planet as a created object considered in itself, but the present human order in rebellion against God. Likewise, in 2 Corinthians 5:17 Paul says, "If anyone is in Christ, he is a new creation. The old has passed away; behold, the new has come." The believer does not cease to exist materially. Rather, the old sinful standing and identity are replaced by a new standing and identity in Christ. That analogy helps clarify Revelation 21. The emphasis is on the decisive end of the old condition and the establishment of the new one.

The former order included all the realities named in Revelation 21:4: tears, death, mourning, crying, and pain. Those things do not belong to God's original purpose for mankind. Genesis 1–2 presents a good creation, life in fellowship with God, and a human pair placed on earth to live under His blessing. Death entered through sin, as Romans 5:12 explains. Therefore, when death is abolished, God is not abandoning His purpose for the earth. He is restoring and completing it. The new earth is the earth as it was always meant to be under Jehovah's rule.

The Sea Was No More

John adds, "and the sea was no more." This clause has often been misunderstood. The point is not primarily geographical, as though the final state depends upon the literal absence of all water. In Revelation, the sea carries symbolic weight. In Revelation 13:1 the beast rises out of the sea. In Revelation 20:13 the sea gives up the dead who were in it. Within the symbolic world of the book, the sea is associated with unrest, separation, hidden danger, and the threatening instability of the old order. For that reason, its removal signifies that everything it represented in relation to death, chaos, and evil has no place in the final creation.

This fits the broader biblical use of sea imagery. Isaiah 57:20 says, "The wicked are like the tossing sea; for it cannot be quiet, and its waters toss up mire and dirt." The sea in Scripture is not always negative in every context, but it frequently serves as a fitting emblem of untamed power and instability. John's point is that the final order is free from every element of menace, separation, and rebellion that characterized the old one. Nothing remains that threatens the peace of God's people.

The New Jerusalem Coming Down From God

Revelation 21:2 says, "And I saw the holy city, new Jerusalem, coming down out of heaven from God, made ready as a bride adorned for her husband." This statement is central to understanding the new heavens and new earth. The city comes down from God. Its source is heavenly and divine. It is not the result of human political reform, religious progress, or moral development. Fallen mankind cannot build the world to come. God must bring it. This stands in direct contrast to Babel in Genesis 11, where men sought to build upward in proud independence. In Revelation 21, the city descends because salvation is from Jehovah.

The city is also called "the bride." That means it is not merely a location. It is the glorified covenant people of God in their perfected relation to the Lamb. Later in Revelation 21:9-10, one of the angels tells John, "Come, I will show you the Bride, the wife of the Lamb," and then shows him the holy city Jerusalem. The city, therefore, is a corporate image. It represents God's people in ordered, glorious, covenant form. This union of city and bride imagery teaches that God's redeemed people are both a community and a dwelling place. They are the people among whom He lives.

This fulfills promises found throughout Scripture. Psalm 132:13-14 says, "For Jehovah has chosen Zion; he has desired it for his dwelling place: 'This is my resting place forever; here I will dwell, for I have desired it.'" Ezekiel 37:26-28 promises that Jehovah will set His sanctuary among His people forevermore and that the nations will know that He sanctifies Israel when His sanctuary is in their midst forever. Revelation 21 presents the final and full realization of that dwelling. What the tabernacle and temple foreshadowed finds its complete expression in the new creation.

The Tabernacle of God Is with Men

The loud voice from the throne in Revelation 21:3 declares, "Behold, the tabernacle of God is with men. He will dwell with them, and they will be his peoples, and God Himself will be with them as their God." This is the theological center of the passage. The greatest blessing of the new heavens and new earth is not first the removal of pain, though that is glorious. It is not first the beauty of the city, though that is magnificent. It is the dwelling of God with redeemed humanity. The covenant formula that echoes through Scripture reaches its consummation here: He will be their God, and they will be His people.

This promise appears in Leviticus 26:11-12, Jeremiah 31:33, and Ezekiel 37:27. In each case, Jehovah identifies the heart of redemption as restored relationship with Himself. Sin brought alienation. Redemption brings nearness. Under the Mosaic arrangement, God dwelt among Israel in a mediated way. There was a tabernacle, then a temple, priestly access, sacrifices, veils, and boundaries. Those institutions were real and divinely appointed, but they were not the final form of God's dwelling with man. Hebrews 9–10 explains that those arrangements pointed forward to a better and final access established through Christ's sacrificial death. Revelation 21 shows the consummation of that access. There is no distance, no exclusion of the redeemed, and no interruption of communion. Jehovah dwells with His people permanently.

This also shows why the final hope cannot be reduced to disembodied existence. God dwells with men. The term is concrete and relational. It means redeemed humanity in its true created form, living under God's favor. The Bible does not present the earth as a temporary mistake to be abandoned, but as the intended sphere of human life under Jehovah. The new earth is therefore the fitting setting for the fulfillment of His promise to dwell with mankind.

The End of Tears, Death, Mourning, Crying, and Pain

Revelation 21:4 is one of the most beloved verses in Scripture: "He will wipe away every tear from their eyes, and death shall be no more, neither shall there be mourning, nor crying, nor pain anymore, for the former things have passed away." Every part of this verse is saturated with redemptive significance. The tenderness of the language matters. God Himself wipes away the tears. The comfort of the new creation is not abstract. It is personal. Jehovah does not merely decree that sorrow is over. He acts toward His people in restoring compassion.

The abolition of death is the great turning point. First Corinthians 15:26 says, "The last enemy to be destroyed is death." Death is not natural in the sense of belonging to God's original purpose for man. It is the wages of sin, as Romans 6:23 teaches. When death is removed, the entire network of experiences that accompany it is also removed. Mourning, crying, and pain belong to a world where death reigns, where bodies weaken, relationships break, persecutions wound, and hope is continually assaulted by the realities of human sin and frailty. In the new creation, those realities are gone because the order that produced them has passed away.

This does not mean that the redeemed forget Jehovah's justice or lose all awareness of what He has done in history. Isaiah 65:17 means that the former things no longer come to mind as sources of grief and burden. Their oppressive force is gone. The misery of the old order no longer presses upon the minds and bodies of God's people. Instead, they live in the settled peace of the completed kingdom.

All Things Made New by the One Seated on the Throne

Revelation 21:5 says, "And He who was seated on the throne said, 'Behold, I am making all things new.'" The one speaking is the sovereign God whose rule has governed the entire Apocalypse from the opening throne vision onward. This declaration matters because it grounds the new creation in divine action. Men do not make all things new. Institutions do not make all things new. Technology does not make all things new. Political power does not make all things new. Jehovah does.

The phrase "all things" is comprehensive. It does not mean that every creature without exception receives eternal life, because Revelation has already distinguished between the redeemed and the condemned. Rather, it means that every part of the order that belongs to God's final kingdom is brought into newness. Nothing remains under the corruption of the old rebellious system. This corresponds with Isaiah's prophecy and with Paul's words in Romans 8 concerning the liberation of creation.

God then commands John to write, "for these words are faithful and true." That assurance is vital. Revelation was written to churches facing pressure, seduction, false teaching, and persecution. What they saw with their eyes might have suggested that beastly power was permanent. The throne says otherwise. The promise of renewal is absolutely reliable because it rests on the character of the One who speaks. Numbers 23:19 states, "God is not man, that he should lie." What He promises, He brings to pass.

The Alpha and the Omega and the Gift of the Water of Life

In Revelation 21:6 God says, "It is done! I am the Alpha and the Omega, the beginning and the end." This declaration means that Jehovah stands at the origin and consummation of His purpose. Nothing frustrates Him. History is not a contest in which God may or may not prevail. He is the One who began all things and the One who completes His redemptive design. Isaiah 46:9-10 similarly records Jehovah's words: "I am God, and there is no other; I am God, and there is none like me, declaring the end from the beginning."

The same verse continues, "To the thirsty I will give from the spring of the water of life without payment." The new creation is received as gift, not purchased by human merit. The thirsty are those who know their need and long for life from God. This promise echoes

Isaiah 55:1: "Come, everyone who thirsts, come to the waters." It also recalls Jesus' words in John 4:14 and John 7:37-38, where living water signifies the life-giving provision that comes from God through Christ. In Revelation, the water of life is the final and unending enjoyment of that divine provision in the consummated order.

The fact that it is given "without payment" underscores grace. Eternal life is not the natural possession of man. It is the gift of God. Man is not inherently immortal. Scripture teaches that everlasting life is granted through God's redemptive work. That is why Revelation can contrast the water of life with the second death. One is the gift God gives. The other is the final penalty borne by those who remain in rebellion.

The Inheritance of the One Who Conquers

Revelation 21:7 says, "The one who conquers will inherit these things, and I will be his God and he will be my son." Throughout Revelation, conquering does not mean establishing earthly dominance by force. It means persevering in faithfulness to God and to Christ despite pressure, suffering, or temptation. The churches in Revelation 2–3 are repeatedly called to conquer. That call frames the entire book. Those who conquer are those who refuse idolatry, reject compromise, endure persecution, and remain loyal to the Lamb.

The inheritance language is rich with biblical meaning. An inheritance is a settled possession granted according to God's promise. In the Old Testament, the land inheritance pointed beyond itself to the larger reality of life under Jehovah's blessing. In the consummation, what is inherited is the full order of the new creation. The conqueror receives the blessings just described: the water of life, the dwelling of God, the end of sorrow, and the permanence of covenant relationship.

The phrase "he will be my son" expresses intimate covenant acceptance. It recalls 2 Samuel 7:14 and the filial language associated with those who belong to God. Here it points to the redeemed person standing in a settled relation of belonging under the favor of Jehovah. This is not a vague universal fatherhood. It is covenant sonship granted to those who belong to Him through redemption.

The Exclusion of the Wicked and the Second Death

Revelation 21:8 provides the contrast: "But as for the cowardly, the faithless, the detestable, as for murderers, the sexually immoral persons, sorcerers, idolaters, and all liars, their portion will be in the lake that burns with fire and sulfur, which is the second death." The new heavens and new earth are not universalistic. They do not blur the line between righteousness and wickedness. Final restoration for the redeemed is accompanied by final exclusion for the wicked.

The list begins with the cowardly because, in Revelation's setting, cowardice means shrinking back from fidelity to Christ under pressure. It is the refusal to stand with the Lamb when loyalty is costly. The rest of the list gathers together the moral world of rebellion. Murder, sexual immorality, sorcery, idolatry, and falsehood are all marks of the old order opposed to Jehovah. Such things cannot enter the new creation because they are contrary to the very character of the holy city.

Most important is the explanation that the lake of fire is "the second death." Scripture interprets Scripture here. The final punishment is defined as death. It is not a second opportunity and not a parallel eternal life in tormenting communion with God. It is the irreversible judicial end of those who reject Him. Revelation 20:14 already identifies the lake of fire as the second death. Thus the contrast in Revelation 21 is absolute: everlasting life in God's renewed order for the redeemed, and final death for the wicked.

The New Creation and the Fulfillment of God's Purpose for the Earth

When all the biblical testimony is gathered together, the new heavens and new earth must be understood as the final realization of Jehovah's purpose for creation. Genesis opens with heaven and earth created by God, man made in His image, and the human pair placed on earth to live under His blessing and exercise responsible dominion. Sin introduced curse, alienation, corruption, and death. Yet God did not abandon His purpose. Through promise, covenant, prophecy, the coming of Christ, His sacrificial death, resurrection, and kingly rule, He moves history toward the restoration and completion of what He intended from the beginning.

The new heavens and new earth are therefore the opposite of defeat. They are the declaration that Jehovah's purpose stands. Psalm 115:16 says, "The heavens are Jehovah's heavens, but the earth he has given to the children of man." Matthew 5:5 declares, "Blessed are the meek, for they shall inherit the earth." These words find their fullest realization in the final renewal. The righteous do not inherit a ruined world left under the effects of sin. They inherit the new earth, the fully renewed sphere of life under God.

This renewed order is also moral in character. Second Peter 3:13 says it is a place "in which righteousness dwells." Righteousness is not merely present as one feature among others. It dwells there. It belongs there. It defines the place. That is why nothing unclean can enter the holy city, as Revelation 21:27 makes clear. The final creation is not a mixed world like the present one. It is wholly suited to the presence of God and the life of His redeemed people.

The Holy City as the Center of the Renewed Order

Revelation 21 goes on to describe the new Jerusalem in great detail because the city represents the perfected covenant community in the final order. Its wall, gates, foundations, measurements, and glory all communicate holiness, security, beauty, and divine design. Particularly striking is Revelation 21:22, where John says, "I saw no temple in the city, for its temple is Jehovah God the Almighty and the Lamb." This means that the old form of mediated worship has given way to direct and permanent communion. The whole city is holy because God's presence fills it entirely.

The city also has no need of sun or moon, "for the glory of God gives it light, and its lamp is the Lamb" (Rev. 21:23). This does not mean creation is abolished into formless spirituality. It means that the deepest source of life, guidance, and glory in the final order is the immediate presence of God shining through the Lamb. Jesus Christ remains central to the entire consummation. Redemption, access, light, and life all remain inseparably bound to Him.

Revelation 21:24-26 speaks of the nations walking by the city's light and bringing their glory into it. This shows that the new creation includes ordered redeemed human life under God's rule. The city is not isolated from the renewed earth. It is the radiant center of divine presence and covenant blessing in relation to the redeemed human order. Everything finds its proper place in relation to Jehovah and the Lamb.

Why This Hope Matters for the Christian Life

The doctrine of the new heavens and new earth is not merely material for theological reflection. It is meant to shape Christian endurance, holiness, worship, and hope. Peter draws this practical implication directly in 2 Peter 3:11-14. Because the present order will give way to the righteous new creation, believers are to live lives of holiness and godliness, waiting for and hastening the coming of the day of God. Future hope is meant to produce present faithfulness.

Likewise, Revelation was given to strengthen churches under pressure. The promise of the new creation tells believers that suffering does not have the last word, persecution does not have the last word, corrupt worldly power does not have the last word, and death does not have the last word. Jehovah does. The One seated on the throne says, "Behold, I am making all things new." Therefore, Christians are called to reject compromise with the present world, endure in loyalty to Christ, and set their minds on the certainty of the coming kingdom.

This hope also guards against despair. The world as now experienced is filled with grief, disease, violence, aging, disappointment, oppression, and death. Scripture does not minimize those realities. Revelation 21 faces them directly. But it places them under the sentence of passing away. They belong to "the former things." They are not permanent. The permanence belongs to God's dwelling, God's city, God's light, and God's life.

The New Heavens and New Earth as the Final Answer of Scripture

From Genesis to Revelation, the Bible moves toward this outcome. Creation begins good, is marred by sin, and is then progressively directed by Jehovah toward restoration through His redemptive acts in history. The prophets announce it. Christ secures it. The resurrection guarantees it. The final judgment clears the way for it. Revelation unveils it. The new heavens and new earth are thus the Bible's final answer to the problem of sin and death in relation to mankind and creation.

Nothing unclean survives there. Nothing false enters there. Nothing painful threatens there. Nothing death-bound remains there. Jehovah dwells there with His people. The Lamb lights the city. The thirsty receive the water of life. The conquerors inherit all these things. The former order is gone, not because God surrendered His purpose, but because He completed it. The new creation is the everlasting order in which His righteousness, holiness, truth, and life are fully and permanently displayed.

Glossary of Terms

Abomination of Desolation

The expression "abomination of desolation" refers to a profaning or desecrating act associated with the end-time crisis described in Daniel and in Jesus' Olivet Discourse. It is not a vague reference to evil or corruption but a specific act of rebellion against God that marks the transition into the final period of severe tribulation. The term describes a decisive moment when something detestable in God's sight intrudes into what is holy, signaling the escalation of lawless opposition to God's rule.

Age, End of the

The "end of the age" refers to the closing of the present order of human rebellion and the transition into the next phase of God's kingdom administration. It does not mean the annihilation of the earth or the disappearance of existence. Rather, it marks the termination of the present corrupt system characterized by deception, injustice, persecution, and resistance to Jehovah. Its end introduces the open manifestation of Christ's righteous authority and the removal of the present rebellious order.

Antichrist

The term "antichrist" describes that which opposes Christ or attempts to replace Him. The word encompasses both present realities and a climactic manifestation of anti-Christ opposition. Scripture speaks of many antichrists already active in the world, demonstrating that the spirit of antichrist has been operating throughout history through denial of Christ's identity, corruption of His teachings, and counterfeit religious authority. The doctrine therefore warns against reducing the concept to only one future individual while ignoring ongoing theological opposition to Christ.

Apocalyptic Language

Apocalyptic language refers to the vivid symbolic style frequently used in prophetic books such as Daniel and Revelation. This language employs dramatic imagery such as beasts, horns, cosmic disturbances, symbolic numbers, and heavenly visions. These symbols are not meaningless fantasy. They communicate real truths through symbolic representation governed by context, grammar, and the broader teaching of Scripture. Proper interpretation respects the symbolic nature of the language while recognizing that the realities described are genuine.

Armageddon

Armageddon refers to the gathering of the kings of the earth for the climactic war described in Revelation as "the war of the great day of God the Almighty." It is not simply a catastrophic war among nations or a general term for global disaster. It represents the final confrontation between rebellious world powers and the authority of God before the establishment of Christ's millennial reign. Armageddon is therefore a theological and judicial event rather than merely a military conflict.

Beast

The beast described in Revelation symbolizes organized anti-God world power that persecutes the people of God and demands allegiance. The imagery draws upon Daniel's visions, where kingdoms are portrayed as beasts because of their violence, arrogance, and rebellion. The beast represents a system of authority characterized by hostility toward God's truth and coercion of human loyalty.

Day of Jehovah / Day of the Lord

The "day of Jehovah" refers to a decisive period in which God intervenes directly in human affairs to judge rebellion and vindicate righteousness. While certain passages apply the expression to historical judgments, its fullest sense appears in the final divine intervention connected with the return of Christ. It represents the exposure of human pride, the collapse of rebellious power, and the triumph of God's authority.

Death

Death is the cessation of conscious human life. Scripture presents death as the loss of life rather than a transition into another form of conscious existence. The dead await resurrection rather than experiencing an ongoing conscious state. Because of this, resurrection becomes essential to the biblical hope. Death is an enemy that must be defeated rather than a friend or liberation from bodily existence.

Eschatology

Eschatology is the branch of theology concerned with the "last things." It includes the study of the end of the age, the return of Christ, resurrection, judgment, the defeat of evil, and the renewal of creation. The subject is not intended to promote speculation but to strengthen faith, encourage perseverance, and provide clarity about God's purposes for history.

False Christ / False Prophet

A false christ is any individual, movement, or teaching that falsely claims authority belonging to Jesus Christ or distorts His identity. A false prophet claims to speak for God while actually spreading deception. These figures play a significant role in end-time deception because their authority is based on counterfeit resemblance to truth rather than open hostility alone.

Gehenna

Gehenna refers to the place of final destruction under divine judgment. It is distinct from Sheol and Hades. While Sheol and Hades relate to the grave and temporary death, Gehenna represents irreversible ruin beyond recovery. It is the final destiny of the wicked rather than a temporary condition.

Great Tribulation

The great tribulation refers to the unprecedented period of distress that occurs immediately before the return of Christ. It represents the culmination of anti-God rebellion and persecution directed against the faithful. Although severe, this period is limited by divine authority and ultimately precedes the vindication of God's people and the overthrow of rebellious powers.

Great White Throne

The great white throne is the final judgment seat described in Revelation. The throne is described as "great" because of its ultimate authority and "white" because of its purity and righteousness. At this judgment the dead are raised and judged according to their deeds, marking the final moral accounting of humanity before the arrival of the new heavens and new earth.

Hades

Hades is the Greek term corresponding to the grave. It represents the state of death rather than a place of eternal conscious punishment. Scripture describes death and Hades as temporary realities that will ultimately be destroyed. The dead are raised from Hades at the resurrection, demonstrating that it is not the final state of humanity.

Historical-Grammatical Method

The historical-grammatical method is the approach to interpreting Scripture that seeks to understand the intended meaning of the biblical authors by examining grammar, context, literary form, and historical background. This method respects the unity of Scripture and avoids speculative interpretation or the imposition of modern theories onto the biblical text.

Holy Ones

The term "holy ones" refers to those set apart for God. In prophetic and apocalyptic contexts it often refers to the faithful people of God who endure persecution from hostile powers but are ultimately vindicated by divine judgment.

Lake of Fire

The lake of fire represents the final judgment described as the "second death." It signifies ultimate destruction under divine judgment. Death, Hades, the devil, and those not found in the book of life are cast into this final state of irreversible judgment.

Last Days

The "last days" describe the final epoch of history beginning with the first coming of Christ and continuing until His return. This period includes the spread of the gospel, increasing opposition to truth, and growing deception leading toward the final crisis at the end of the age.

Man of Lawlessness

The man of lawlessness described in 2 Thessalonians represents the concentration of rebellion against God within the sphere of worship. He exalts himself and promotes deception through counterfeit signs and falsehood. His influence culminates in opposition to Christ but is ultimately destroyed by Christ's appearing.

Mark of the Beast

The mark of the beast represents identification with and allegiance to the rebellious system symbolized by the beast. It signifies participation in a system that opposes God and demands loyalty. The mark symbolizes ownership and worship—whether allegiance belongs to God or to the beastly order.

Millennium

The millennium refers to the thousand-year reign of Christ described in Revelation 20. It follows the defeat of the beast and precedes the final judgment. During this period Christ exercises authority before the ultimate defeat of evil and the transition to the final new creation.

Prophecy

Prophecy is divine revelation delivered through inspired messengers. It may include prediction, but its purpose extends beyond foretelling events. Prophecy exposes sin, calls people to repentance, reveals divine judgment, and provides assurance of God's future purposes.

Rapture

The term "rapture" refers to the gathering of believers associated with the return of Christ. It is connected with resurrection and the visible coming of Christ rather than a secret or hidden event. The concept must be understood within the larger biblical teaching concerning Christ's return and the resurrection of the dead.

Resurrection

Resurrection is the act by which God raises the dead to life. It is central to biblical hope because it demonstrates victory over death. Resurrection restores life to those who have died and prepares them either for eternal life or for judgment.

Second Death

The second death is the final and irreversible destruction described in Revelation. It is identified with the lake of fire and represents the ultimate judgment from which there is no resurrection.

Sheol

Sheol is the Old Testament term referring to the grave or the realm of the dead. Those in Sheol are described as inactive and unconscious, awaiting resurrection rather than experiencing ongoing life.

Signs of the End of the Age

The signs described by Jesus include deception, wars, upheavals, persecution, apostasy, and the proclamation of the gospel. These developments mark the progression toward the final crisis before Christ's return. Their purpose is to encourage vigilance and faithfulness rather than speculation.

Time of the End

The "time of the end" refers to the intensified period immediately preceding the culmination of history. During this period opposition to God reaches its climax and divine judgment approaches its fulfillment.

Unevangelized

The unevangelized refers to those who have not received the gospel message. The subject is discussed in connection with divine justice, resurrection, and final judgment, affirming that God judges righteously.

Watchfulness

Watchfulness describes the attitude believers must maintain in light of Christ's return. It involves readiness, discernment, faithfulness, and perseverance rather than fear or speculation.

New Heavens and New Earth

The new heavens and new earth describe the final renewal of creation in which death, sorrow, and corruption are removed. God dwells with humanity, and the former order of suffering and rebellion is replaced with everlasting righteousness and life.

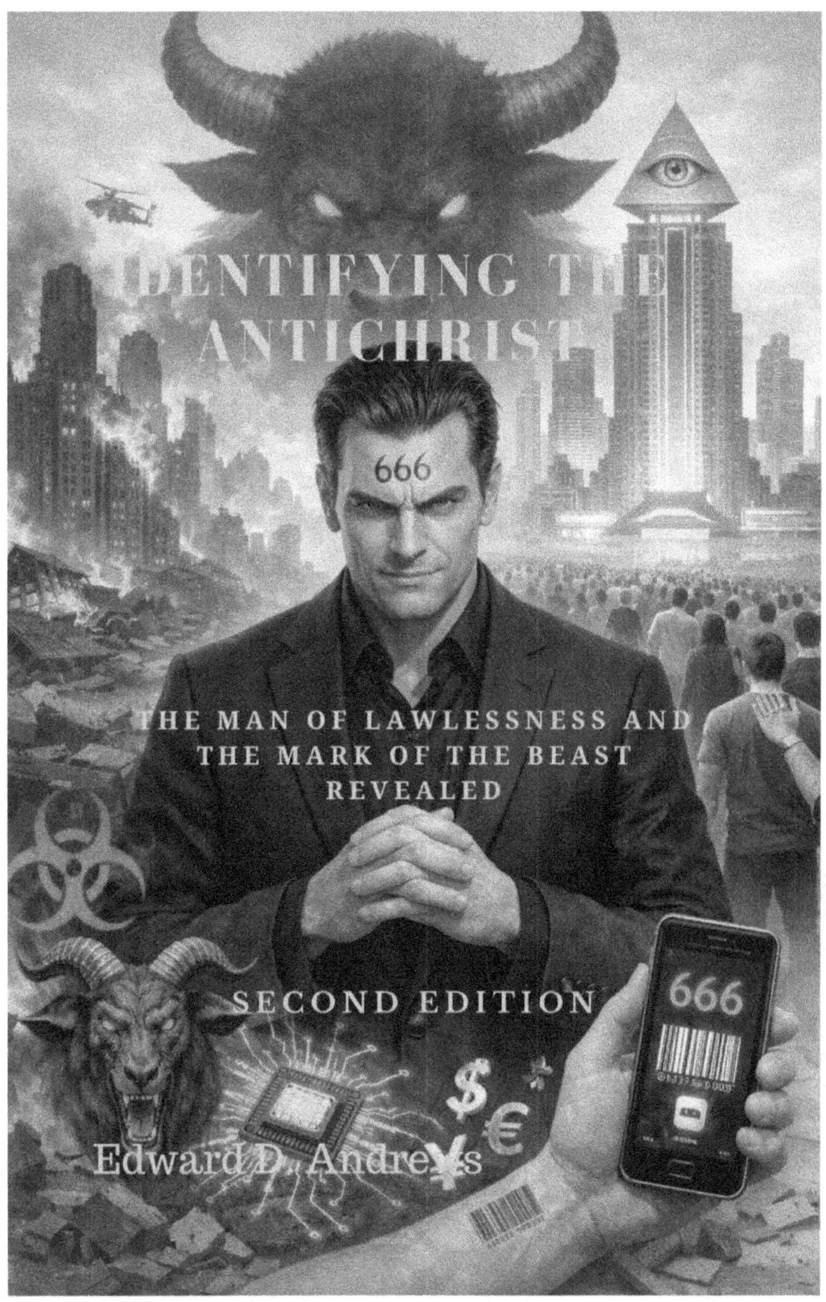
666
THE MAN OF LAWLESSNESS AND
THE MARK OF THE BEAST
REVEALED
SECOND EDITION
666

SECOND EDITION
THE SECOND COMING OF CHRIST
BASIC BIBLE DOCTRINES OF THE CHRISTIAN FAITH
Edward D. Andrews

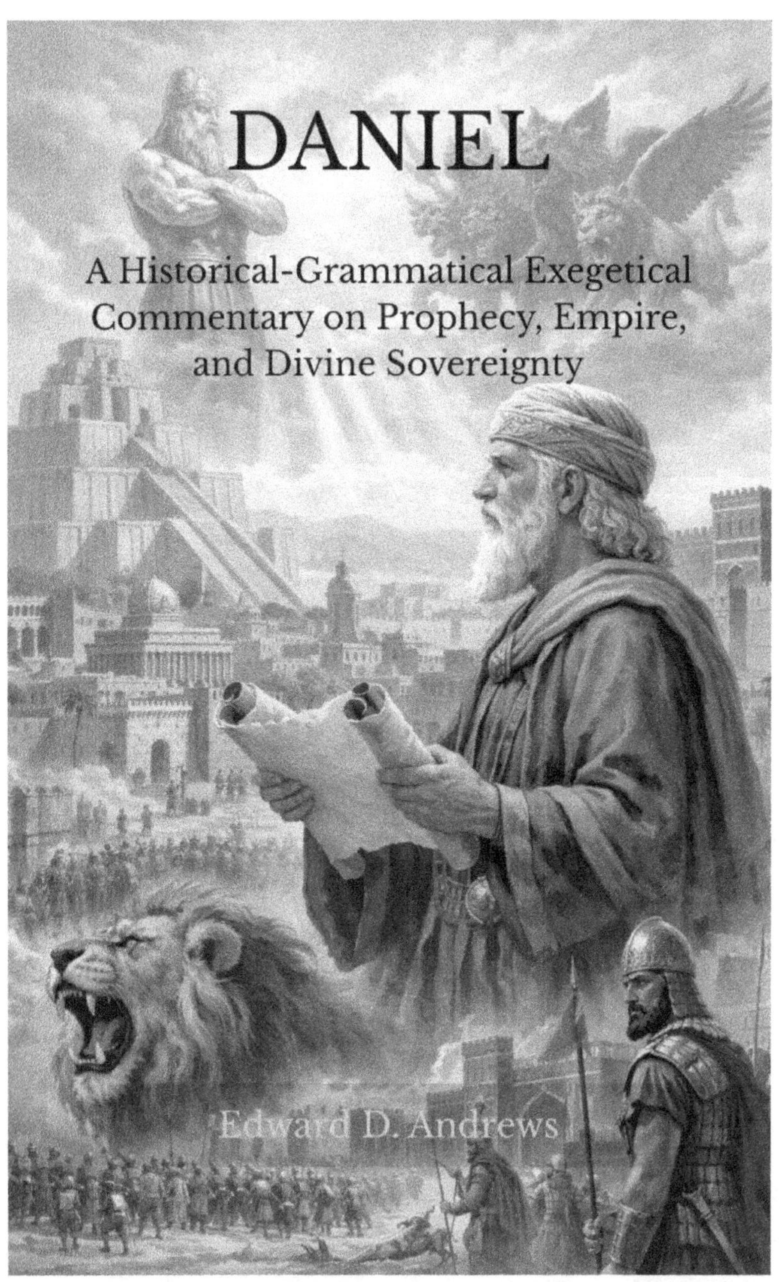
DANIEL
A Historical-Grammatical Exegetical Commentary on Prophecy, Empire, and Divine Sovereignty
Edward D. Andrews

Edward D. Andrews
REVELATION
A Historical-Grammatical Exegetical
Commentary on the Apocalypse, the Kingdom
of God, and the Final Triumph of God

Bibliography

Akin, D. L. (2001). *The New American Commentary: 1, 2, 3 John.* Nashville, TN: Broadman & Holman .

Aland, K., Black, M., & Martini, C. M. (1993; 2006). *The Greek New Testament, Fourth Revised Edition (Interlinear With Morphology).* Deutsche Bibelgesellschaft: United Bible Society.

Andrews, E. D. (2016). *EXPLAINING THE DOCTRINE OF SALVATION: Basic Bible Doctrines of the Christian Faith.* Cambridge, OH: Christian Publishing House.

Andrews, E. D. (2016). *INTERPRETING THE BIBLE: Introduction to Biblical Hermeneutics.* Cambridge, OH: Christian Publishing House.

Andrews, E. D. (2016). *WHAT IS HELL?: Basic Bible Doctrines of the Christian Faith.* Cambridge, OH: Christian Publishing House.

Andrews, E. D. (2017). *FEARLESS: Be Courageous and Strong Through Your Faith In These Last Days.* Cambridge, OH: Christian Publishing House.

Andrews, E. D. (2017). *GOD WILL GET YOU THROUGH THIS: Hope and Help for Your Difficult Times.* Cambridge, OH: Christian Publishing House.

Andrews, E. D. (2017). *HOW TO STUDY YOUR BIBLE: Rightly Handling the Word of God.* Cambridge, OH: Christian Publishing House.

Andrews, E. D. (2017). *HUMAN IMPERFECTION: While We Were Sinners Christ Died For Us.* Cambridge, OH: Christian Ppublishing House.

Andrews, E. D. (2017). *IDENTIFYING THE ANTICHRIST: The Man of Lawlessness and the Mark of the Beast Revealed.* Cambridge, OH: Christian Publishing House.

Andrews, E. D. (2018). *BLESSED BY GOD IN SATAN'S WORLD: How All Things Are Working for Your Good.* Cambridge, OH: Christian Publishing House.

Andrews, E. D. (2018). *REASONABLE FAITH: Saving Those Who Doubt.* Cambridge, OH: Christian Publishing House.

Andrews, E. D. (2018). *REASONING FROM THE SCRIPTURES: Sharing CHRIST as You Help Others to Learn about the Mighty works of God.* Cambridge, Ohio: Christian Publishing House.

Andrews, E. D. (2019). *SATAN: Know Your Enemy.* Cambridge, OH: Christian Publishing House.

Andrews, E. D. (2023). *BIBLICAL APOCALYPTICS HANDBOOK: A Study of the Most Important Revelations that God and Christ Disclosed in the Bible.* Cambridge, OH: Christian Publishing House.

Andrews, E. D. (2023). *BIBLICAL EXEGESIS: Biblical Criticism on Trial.* Cambridge, OH: Christian Publishing House.

Andrews, E. D. (2023). *CHRISTIAN APOLOGETICS: Answering the Tough Questions: Evidence and Reason in Defense of the Faith.* Cambridge, Ohio: Christian Publishing House.

Andrews, E. D. (2023). *HOW WE GOT THE BIBLE.* Cambridge, OH: Christian Publishing House.

Andrews, E. D. (2024). *CHRISTIAN THEOLOGY: The Christian's Ultimate Guide to Learning from the Bible.* Cambridge, OH: Christian Publishing House.

Andrews, E. D. (2024). *HELL: All You Need to Know About Hell.* Cambridge, OH: Christian Publishing House.

Andrews, E. D. (2024). *REASON MEETS FAITH: Addressing and Refuting Atheism's Challenges to Christianity.* Cambridge, OH: Christian Publishing House.

Andrews, E. D. (2025). *A FRESH LOOK AT PAUL'S THEOLOGY: Biblical Theology as Revealed through Paul.* Cambridge, OH: Christian Publishing House.

Andrews, E. D. (2025). *BIBLICAL WORDS AND THEIR MEANING: An Introduction to Lexical Semantics.* Cambridge, OH: Christian Publishing House.

Andrews, E. D. (2025). *CAN WE TRUST THE BIBLE?* Cambridge, OH: Christian Publishing House.

Andrews, E. D. (2025). *IMMORTALITY OF THE SOUL: The Birth of the Doctrine.* Cambridge, OH: Christian Publishing House.

Andrews, E. D. (2025). *THE ANDREWS BIBLE BLUEPRINT: Unlocking Scripture's Truth, History, and Wisdom.* Cambridge, OH: Christian Publishing House.

Andrews, E. D. (2025). *THE APOSTLE PAUL: Teacher, Preacher, Apologist, and Evangelist.* Cambridge, OH: Christian Publishing House.

Andrews, E. D. (2025). *THE GUIDE TO SPIRITUAL WARFARE: Standing Firm in the Armor of God Against the Schemes of the Devil.* Cambridge, OH: Christian Publishing House.

Andrews, E. D. (2025). *THE LAST WATCHMAN: Standing for Truth in a Fallen World.* Cambridge, OH: Christian Publishing House.

Andrews, E. D. (2025). *THE WAR AGAINST THE TRUTH: Exposing the Lies That Allegedly Undermine the Christian Faith.* Cambridge, OH: Christian Publishing House.

Andrews, E. D. (2026). *DANIEL: A Historical-Grammatical Exegetical Commentary on Prophecy, Empire, and Divine Sovereignty.* Cambridge, OH: Christian Publishing House.

Andrews, E. D. (2026). *REVELATION: A Historical-Grammatical Exegetical Commentary on the Apocalypse, the Kingdom of God, and the Final Triumph of God.* Cambridge, OH: Christian Publishing House.

Barnes, A. (1884-85). *Barnes On Revelation: Albert Barnes' Notes On The Whole Bible.* London: Blackie & Son.

Collins, ,. J. (1994). *Daniel: A Commentary on the Book of Daniel.* Minneapolis, MN: Fortress Press.

Easley, K. H. (1999). *Holman New Testament Commentary - Revelation (Volume 12).* Nashville, TN: Broadman & Holman.

Ian, P. (2018). *Revelation: An Introduction and Commentary (Volume 20).* Downers Grove, Il: InterVarsity Press.

Miller, S. (1994). *Daniel (New American Commentary, 18).* Nashville, TN: Broadman & Holman Reference.

Thomas, R. L. (1992). *Revelation 1-7: An Exegetical Commentary*. Chicago, IL: Moody Publishers.

Thomas, R. L. (1995). *Revelation 8-22: An Exegetical Commentary* . Chicago, IL: Moody Publishers.

Walvoord, J. F. (2012). *Daniel (The John Walvoord Prophecy Commentaries).* Chicago, IL: Moody Publishers.

www.ingramcontent.com/pod-product-compliance
Lightning Source LLC
LaVergne TN
LVHW011223080426
835509LV00005B/281

* 9 7 8 0 6 9 2 6 6 9 8 9 1 *